SEW&GO

EASY CONVERTIBLE PROJECTS FOR THE ACTIVE LIFESTYLE

OTHER BOOKS AVAILABLE FROM CHILTON   *Robbie Fanning, Series Editor*

CONTEMPORARY QUILTING

All Quilt Blocks Are Not Square, by Debra Wagner

Barbara Johannah's Crystal Piecing

The Complete Book of Machine Quilting, Second Edition, by Robbie and Tony Fanning

Contemporary Quilting Techniques, by Pat Cairns

Creative Triangles for Quilters, by Janet B. Elwin

Dye It! Paint It! Quilt It!, by Joyce Mori and Cynthia Myerberg

Fast Patch, by Anita Hallock

Precision Pieced Quilts Using the Foundation Method, by Jane Hall and Dixie Haywood

The Quilter's Guide to Rotary Cutting, by Donna Poster

Scrap Quilts Using Fast Patch, by Anita Hallock

Stars Galore and Even More, by Donna Poster

Stitch 'n' Quilt, by Kathleen Eaton

Super Simple Quilts, by Kathleen Eaton

Three-Dimensional Pieced Quilts, by Jodie Davis

CRAFT KALEIDOSCOPE

The Banner Book, Ruth Ann Lowery

The Crafter's Guide to Glues, by Tammy Young

Creating and Crafting Dolls, by Eloise Piper and Mary Dilligan

Fabric Crafts and Other Fun with Kids, by Susan Parker Beck and Charlou Lunsford

Quick and Easy Ways with Ribbon, by Ceci Johnson

Learn Bearmaking, by Judi Maddigan

Stamping Made Easy, by Nancy Ward

CREATIVE MACHINE ARTS

ABCs of Serging, by Tammy Young and Lori Bottom

Affordable Heirlooms, by Edna Powers and Gaye Kriegel

Alphabet Stitchery by Hand & Machine, by Carolyn Vosburg Hall

The Button Lover's Book, by Marilyn Green

Claire Shaeffer's Fabric Sewing Guide

The Complete Book of Machine Embroidery, by Robbie and Tony Fanning

Craft an Elegant Wedding, by Tammy Young and Naomi Baker

Distinctive Serger Gifts and Crafts, by Naomi Baker and Tammy Young

Gail Brown's All-New Instant Interiors

Hold It! How to Sew Bags, Totes, Duffels, Pouches, and More, by Nancy Restuccia

How to Make Soft Jewelry, by Jackie Dodson

Innovative Serging, by Gail Brown and Tammy Young

The New Creative Serging Illustrated, by Pati Palmer, Gail Brown, and Sue Green

A New Serge in Wearable Art, by Ann Boyce

Quick Napkin Creations, by Gail Brown

Second Stitches: Recycle as You Sew, by Susan Parker

Serge a Simple Project, by Tammy Young and Naomi Baker

Serge Something Super for Your Kids, by Cindy Cummins

Sew Any Patch Pocket, by Claire Shaeffer

Sew Any Set-In Pocket, by Claire Shaeffer

Sew Sensational Gifts, by Naomi Baker and Tammy Young

Sewing and Collecting Vintage Fashions, by Eileen MacIntosh

Shirley Botsford's Daddy's Ties

Soft Gardens: Make Flowers with Your Sewing Machine, by Yvonne Perez-Collins

The Stretch & Sew Guide to Sewing Knits, by Ann Person

Twenty Easy Machine-Made Rugs, by Jackie Dodson

The Ultimate Serger Answer Guide, by Naomi Baker, Gail Brown and Cindy Kacynski

KNOW YOUR SERGER SERIES, BY TAMMY YOUNG AND NAOMI BAKER

Know Your baby lock

SEW & SERGE SERIES, BY JACKIE DODSON AND JAN SAUNDERS

Sew & Serge Pillows! Pillows! Pillows!

Sew & Serge Terrific Textures

StarWear

Dazzle, by Linda Fry Kenzle

Embellishments, by Linda Fry Kenzle

Jan Saunders' Wardrobe Quick-Fixes

Make It Your Own, by Lori Bottom and Ronda Chaney

Mary Mulari's Garments with Style

A New Serge in Wearable Art, by Ann Boyce

Pattern-Free Fashions, by Mary Lee Trees Cole

Shirley Adams' Belt Bazaar

Sweatshirts with Style, by Mary Mulari

TEACH YOURSELF TO SEW BETTER, BY JAN SAUNDERS

A Step-by-Step Guide to Your New Home

A Step-by-Step Guide to Your Sewing Machine

SEW & GO

EASY CONVERTIBLE PROJECTS FOR THE ACTIVE LIFESTYLE

JASMINE HUBBLE

Chilton

BOOK COMPANY

Radnor, Pennsylvania

Cover design by Anthony Jacobson
Text designed by Lisa Palmer
Illustrations by Ruth Griffin
Photos by Kevin Candland
Sewing by Catharine Anderson

Manufactured in the United States of America

Library of Congress Cataloging in Publication Data
Hubble, Jasmine.
    Sew and go : easy convertible projects for
the active lifestyle / Jasmine Hubble.
        p. cm. — (Creative machine arts)
    Includes index.
    ISBN 0-8019-8658-3 (pbk.)
    1. Sewing. 2. Travel—Equipment and
supplies. I. Title.
    II. Series: Creative machine arts series.
    TT715.H83 1996
    95-48895
    646.2—dc20   CIP

2 3 4 5 6 7 8 9 0 5 4 3 2 1 0 9 8 7 6

The following are registered trademark names
used in this book: *HeatnBond, Lycra, Mylar,
Nylon, Rigilene, The Snap Queen, Supplex,
Teflon, Thinsulite, Ultrex, Velcro,* and *Wonder-
Under.*

Are you interested in a quarterly newsletter
about creative uses of the sewing machine,
serger, and knitting machine? Write to The
Creative Machine-s, PO Box 2634, Menlo Park,
CA 94026.

*To Mom and Dad,
two of the greatest travelers ever*

CONTENTS

Introduction

When I was nine months old, my parents took me on a trip to Arizona. The plan was to put me in a basket strapped to a donkey and take me down into the Grand Canyon! I should have known then that travel was going to be a major part of my life. Not only do I take more than twenty-five business trips a year all across the United States, but my own two children are frequent flyers, who logged in over 100,000 miles each by the time they turned five.

While on the road my family and I have discovered two interesting things about traveling. First, there are two kinds of travelers in the world: those who like adventure and those who don't like surprises. For example, we went camping with some friends and I was responsible for making the coffee. When morning rolled along I found that I had forgotten to pack the drip filter. I looked around and discovered that our dog had chewed holes in the bottom of a plastic Tupperware cup. As far as I was concerned, after it was washed it made the perfect drip filter. Needless to say, our friends couldn't handle it on top of the other surprises they hadn't planned on, such as poison ivy and fog, so they packed up and left without having coffee. (We're all still the best of friends, though, and they have tried camping since and even like it.)

Our second discovery would have taken care of the problem in the first discovery, what this book is all about: having things ready to go. What stops many of us from going places is the thought of packing. Today's hectic pace deprives us of being spontaneous. For instance, if the car was all loaded and all you had to do was get in, you might choose to go on a picnic. This book is full of things to sew—from laundry kits to beach bags that turn inside out into towels to picnic blankets—that are ready to go! You don't need to think about packing because everything you need is already packed. If you stow them in convenient places such as your car, then you can do things at the drop of a hat. Remember that keeping your hands free makes for a more enjoyable trip. Also, don't load yourself down like a packhorse. Teach your kids to carry their own things right from the start. If you sew backpacks and pouches to their garments, they can carry their own jackets and other things with ease.

You will find three types of patterns at the back of the book.

Full-size patterns: These are ready to go and can be cut out as is.

Negative templates: These are full-size pieces to position on fabric for cutting out, but the fabric removed is discarded.

Templates: These get transferred to the garment or item for cutting or sewing lines.

Illustrated instructions will guide you step by step through the sewing process. Watch for the explanation at the beginning of each project telling you which is the right and wrong side of the fabric, towel, interfacing, etc.

All seams are $^1/_4$ inch (6mm) unless otherwise indicated. See Resources for some of the items used in the projects. Other items can be obtained at hardware stores, drugstores, and office supply stores.

Enjoy your next trip and sew to go!

Jasmine Hubble

CHAPTER 1

PACKING LIGHT BUT RIGHT

CONVENIENCE KITS

Laundry Kit

The most important thing to pack is your laundry kit. It will allow you to travel indefinitely with only a carry-on bag! Did you ever wash out a garment in your hotel and reach for one of those funny-looking clothes hangers? They have no hooks, so you can't drip-dry anything over the tub. Following the instructions for making the bag for the Laundry Kit is a list of items to put in it. You'll never be caught short again.

✓ Materials

○ ⅜ yards (31cm) of Ultrex or other waterproof-type fabric

○ Two snaps

Directions

❶ Cut two fronts and two backs (Fig. 1–1), using the patterns at the back of the book. If you wish to monogram your kit, then do this on one of the front sections prior to sewing.

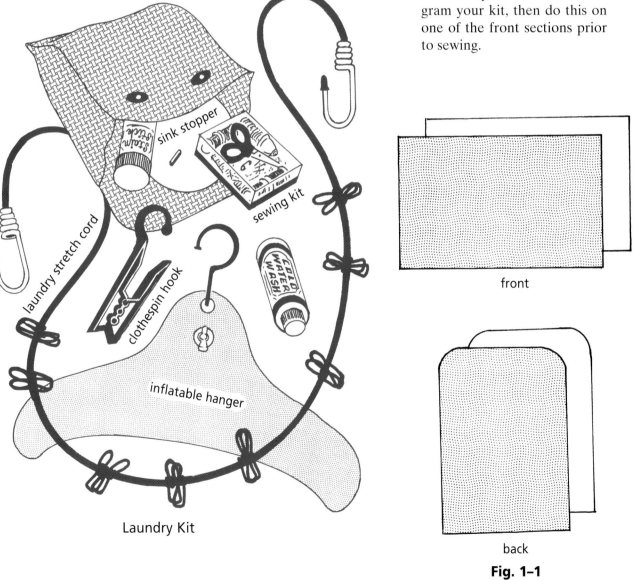

Laundry Kit

front

back

Fig. 1–1

2 With right sides together, sew the two fronts together, leaving an opening between dots for turning. Repeat for the two backs (Fig. 1–2).

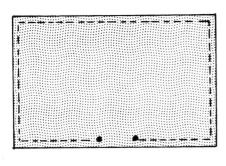

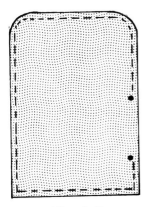

Fig. 1–2

3 Clip curves and corners. Turn right side out, tuck in opening seam allowances and press. Topstitch across the upper edge of the front piece (Fig. 1–3). This is the laundry pouch.

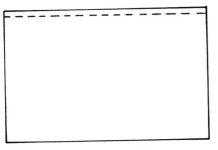

laundry pouch

Fig. 1–3

4 Place the front on top of the back, matching the sides. Stitch sides starting at the bottom of one end and going all the way around the flap of the back piece and down the other side (Fig. 1–4).

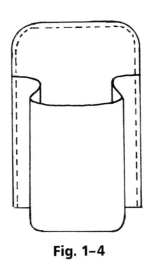

Fig. 1–4

5 Pleat the sides in so that they are even with the bottom of the bag. Stitch across the bottom (Fig. 1–5).

Fig. 1–5

6 Fill bag to locate snap positions. Affix two snaps on the bag (Fig. 1–6). This makes a terrific gift item and can be personalized with the recipient's initials.

Fig. 1–6

Below are the items you should always keep in your Laundry Kit:

- Laundry stretch cord with clips for stretching over the tub or from tree to tree.

- Flat rubber sink stopper in case the sink won't hold water

- Laundry stick for stain removal

- One inflatable clothes hanger to hang knits and sweaters

- Small bottle of liquid laundry soap (dissolves quickly in cold water)

- Hotel sewing kit for emergency mending

The best part about your laundry kit is that you *never* have to unpack it and that it's always ready for your next trip.

TIP

To prevent bottles from leaking try creating a vacuum by:

- *Filling bottle ½ inch (12mm) shy of being full*

- *Squeezing out air and closing top before letting go*

PICNIC BLANKET CAR KIT

Every car should be equipped with one of these. First it's a bag, then it's a blanket! The bag portion is large enough to allow you to pack your own food or to run into the store and fill it up with goodies. If you keep it stocked with paper plates and napkins, you can make spur-of-the-moment picnic decisions. Following are instructions for two sizes. A version that uses 60-inch- (150cm) wide fabric is perfect for a picnic for two or three. The 45-inch- (112.5cm) wide version calls for twice the length; you will have to seam it together down the middle. This size is good for a picnic for four to six. So, depending on the size of your gang, choose the size right for you.

Keep this picnic bag/blanket in your car at all times. After a quick trip to the grocery store, you're all ready for a meal "out."

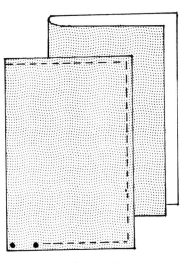

Fig. 1–7

You're never without a blanket for impromptu, last minute picnics.

✓Materials

You will need two kinds of fabric for the blanket: a dark fabric for the side that faces the ground and a fun, lively print for the top side. If you use 45-inch- (112.5cm) wide fabric, don't forget to sew the two lengths together. You will also need 1-inch-wide (2.5cm) webbing for the straps.

Picnic for two or three:
❍ 2¼ yards (2m) of 60-inch- (150cm) wide dark fabric for bottom of blanket and 2¼ yards (2m) of 60-inch- (150cm) wide printed fabric for top of blanket

Picnic for four to six:
❍ 4½ yards (137cm) of 45-inch- (112.5cm) wide dark fabric for bottom of blanket and 4½ yards (137cm) of 45-inch (112.5cm) wide print for top of blanket

For either size:
❍ 3 yards (2.7m) of 1-inch- (2.5cm) wide nylon webbing
❍ 1 yard (90cm) of 45-inch- (112.5cm) wide fabric for bag
❍ Interfacing for ironing to bag piece for extra stability and sturdiness (optional)

Trim the two blanket pieces and bag piece so that they are even and square at the top. This means the top is at a 90-degree angle to the sides. If you are using 45-inch- (112.5cm) wide fabric, seam the two lengths together first and then even the top edge.

Directions

❶ Fold bag piece right sides together along existing fold. Sew all around leaving an opening for turning just before the fold (Fig. 1–7). Clip corners, turn, and press.

❷ Topstitch across both ends closing the opening at the same time. Fold bag in half and press with an iron to form a crease (Fig. 1–8).

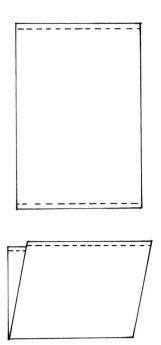

Fig. 1–8

3 Unfold creased bag. Pin straps 5½ inches (13.5cm) in from the sides and starting at the crease. Allow a 33-inch (82.5cm) handle or less on both sides. End back where you started. Sew each side of the strap to the bag. Set bag aside (Fig. 1–9).

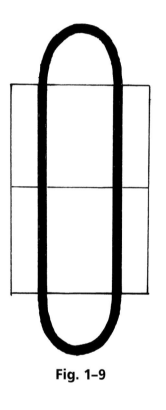

Fig. 1–9

4 If your blanket pieces are from 45-inch- (112.5cm) wide fabric, seam the two lengths together first. With right sides together, sew around the two large blanket pieces, leaving a small opening for turning (Fig. 1–10). Turn and press. Topstitch around the blanket edge, and close the opening.

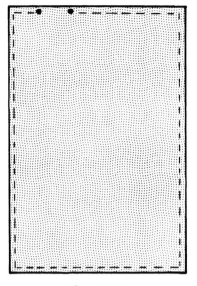

Fig. 1–10

5 Place unfolded bag on top of the underside of the blanket in the upper-left-hand corner and with bag edge flush with blanket edge and strap side facing up. Topstitch across the top (Fig. 1–11).

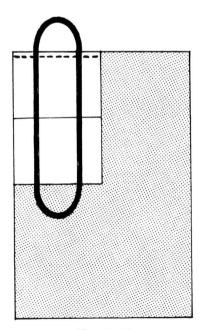

Fig. 1–11

6 Fold bag in half (straps inside), and pin left side even with blanket side. Smooth and pin bag bottom and right side in place. Sew the three bag sides to the blanket (Fig. 1–12).

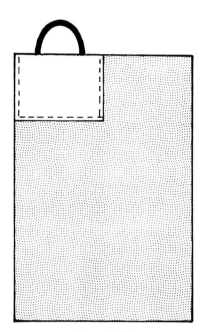

Fig. 1–12

7 To get blanket into the bag, fold the blanket in half the long way and then fold the lower edge up toward the bag. Push blanket through the bottom of the bag, turning it right side out (Fig. 1–13).

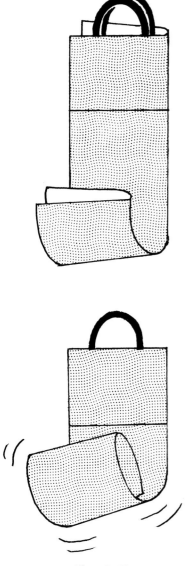

Fig. 1–13

BUNDLE PACKING METHOD

The bundle packing method avoids creating sharp creases in your clothing and void spaces in your luggage, which maximizes what you can fit into a space. This method starts with a suitcase or carry-on bag that has a frame that retains its shape. If you choose the carry-on version, you may want to go with the maximum tolerated size for airlines, which means that it must fit under the seat in front of you.

Before you start packing your clothes keep two things in mind: climate and function. Ask yourself about the climate first, and then choose the appropriate clothing for protection from the elements. Next, choose clothing and accessories to serve you in a variety of social situations.

Start packing the largest items first, then pack the smaller items, followed by clothes that wrinkle less, such as cotton sweaters. The very center of the bag contains a solid core of bathroom essentials. For example, start with a blazer or sports coat. Place it in the suitcase face up. Push it all the way to the back edge and use your hands to mold it into the shape from edge to edge. Let the sleeves and length simply hang over the edges for now. The next item goes on top, but place the item flush with the front instead of the back edge and allow any excess to drape out. The next piece goes flush with the left side, and the next piece is flush with the right side, always allowing sleeves and length to drape over the edges. Continue alternating

TIP

For business trips, you can leave clothing on their hangers in the dry-cleaning bags and pack using the same method. The bags will create an air pocket, allowing the clothes to arrive at your destination less wrinkled. It will take just seconds to hang everything up!

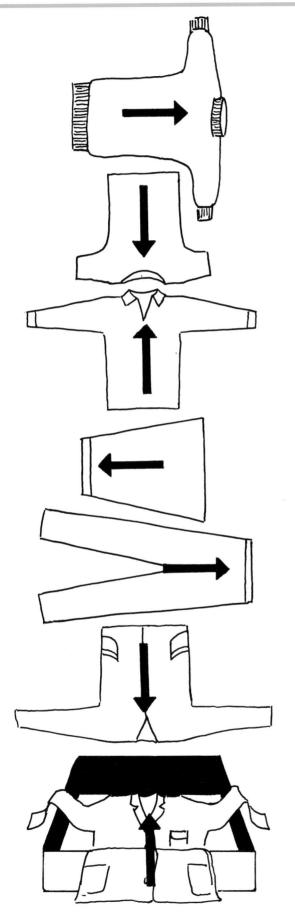

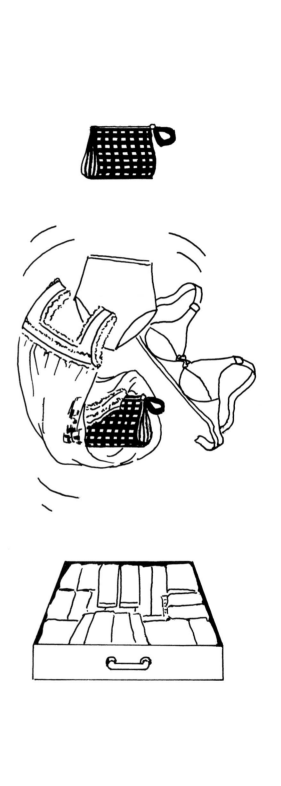

with slacks, skirts, shirts, blouses, and sweaters in this fashion. By doing this you are accomplishing three things:

1. You are distributing double thicknesses such as collars evenly.

2. You are always molding the clothing into the existing shape and avoiding dead space.

3. When you fold sleeves and lengths in, the clothing won't form any sharp creases.

Take your toiletries and wrap your nightshirt and underwear around them, and then place this in the center. Now alternate folding the garments in over the core. You will truly be amazed at the amount of clothing you can pack and the condition it arrives in.

OTHER KITS

Try customizing kits for your own special needs. If you find yourself needing, wishing for, or missing the same items over and over again, put these in a kit. Stow the kits where they can go along for the ride, such as in the glove box, the trunk, under the seat, a suitcase, or a purse, and you won't have to worry about them again.

Here's a list of kits that might make life easier.

Hotel child proofing kit
First aid
Picnic
Entertainment
Hair care
Disaster/earthquake
Medicine
Sewing
Car trips
CDs
Dry clothing

Here are advantages to organizing things in kits:

- You always know where things are and when you reach for certain items, you won't disrupt everything else.

- Messy items remain contained, so fewer spills occur.

- Kits require less space.

- There is less packing and unpacking.

HATS TO GO

TRAVEL HATS

Hats can be important items to pack, especially when prolonged sun exposure is involved. However, they can also be very frustrating items to pack. Here's how you can create a few fun and practical hats that won't cause any packing problems.

THE FLAT HAT

This *no sew* version fits perfectly in the bottom of a suitcase or rolled up in a purse. The cut-out louvers keep your head from overheating and your hair from matting and give the hat its shape.

This no-sew hat is easy to make and take
just about anywhere.

✓Materials

- ❍ Two fabric squares 20 × 20 inches (50 × 50cm) (For reversible hat choose two different fabrics.)
- ❍ 1¼ yards (112cm) extra-heavy HeatnBond
- ❍ 1¼ yards (112cm) heavy fusible interfacing
- ❍ Sharp razor blade or scissors with a point
- ❍ Thumbtack
- ❍ String
- ❍ Pencil

Directions

1 Fuse interfacing to wrong side of both fabric squares. Fuse HeatnBond on top of interfacing on both squares (Fig. 2–1). Peel paper protector sheets from HeatnBond and make a "sandwich," fusing the two squares together (Fig. 2-2).

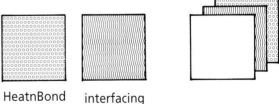

HeatnBond   interfacing

Fig. 2–1

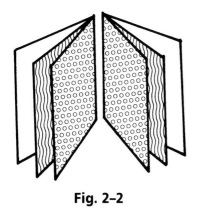

Fig. 2–2

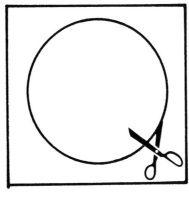

Fig. 2–4

To enlarge the hat, cut the lines longer in the direction of the brim. Wear the hat from either side. Make the hat to match your other travel accessories.

TIP

You can transfer a drawing by making a photocopy of it and then ironing it to the circle with a dry iron. Try this with the template for this project.

❷ Using a thumbtack, string, and a pencil, make a circle on the stabilized fabric square 16 inches (40cm) in diameter (Fig. 2–3).

❹ Transfer the Flat Hat template from the back of the book to the circle and mark the cutting lines (Fig. 2–5). Cut along these lines through all layers with a sharp blade or a pair of sharp scissors.

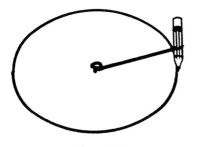

Fig. 2–3

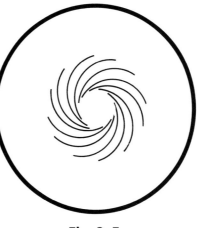

Fig. 2–5

❸ Cut out the circle (Fig. 2–4).

Bandanna Visor

Any bandanna can be turned into a hat with clear plastic and bias tape!

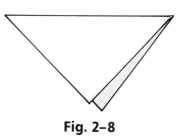

Fig. 2–8

4 Sew visor to the center of the double-folded side of the triangle using a ¼-inch (6mm) overlap (Fig. 2–9).

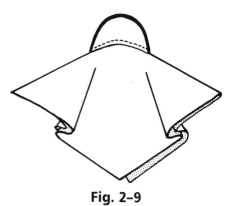

Fig. 2–9

✓ Materials

- ○ One large bandanna or scarf to fit your head, or sew a scarf 24 × 24 inches (60 x 60cm)
- ○ Clear plastic vinyl approx. 20 × 20 inches (50 × 50cm) (Note: You can cut this from clear plastic report covers available at stationery stores and print shops. For extra sturdiness, cut out two and double it.)
- ○ Bias tape to match

Directions

1 Use pattern from the back of the book to cut out plastic visor (Fig. 2–6). Note: there are two different sizes, children's and adult's.

2 Sew bias tape all around plastic visor starting and ending

at the X shown in figure and tucking the end of the tape under (Fig. 2–7).

Fig. 2–6

Fig. 2–7

3 With right side out, fold bandanna or scarf in half to form a triangle (Fig. 2–8).

You can wear your Bandanna Visor two different ways: roll the bandanna up and wear it like a sweatband, or tie it like a kerchief.

Pop-Up Travel Hat and Case

This pop-up hat collapses and can be kept in a handy matching travel case.

✓Materials

- ❍ 1 yard (90 cm) of 45-inch-(112.5cm) wide fabric
- ❍ 3⅓ yards (3m) of sew-through Rigilene polyester boning ½ inch (12mm) wide
- ❍ One 9-to-12-inch (22.5 to 30cm) nylon dress zipper

Preparation

Hat

- Cut one brim 18 inches (45cm) in diameter. Cut out an inner circle 7½ inches (18.75cm) in diameter (Fig. 2–10). You can use a pencil and a string to create the circles (see Flat Hat, Step 2).

Fig. 2–10

- Cut six hat sections (and six more sections if you choose to line it) from the pattern at the back of the book.
- Cut a piece of bias tape 1¾ inches (4.4cm) wide and 58 inches (1.45m) long.
- Cut 2 chin straps 30 inches (75cm) long and 1¼ inches (3.2cm) wide.

Case

- Cut two circles 10 inches (25cm) in diameter.
- Cut one strap 2½ inches (6.25cm) wide and 40 inches (1m) long.
- Cut one gusset 1¾ inches (4.4cm) wide and 32 inches (80cm) long.

Directions

Hat

1 Sew three hat sections together to form a half circle. Repeat with the remaining sections to create four half circles (two for hat and two for lining). Sew two half circles together to make a cap (Fig. 2–11). Repeat for lining. Optional: For a more professional-looking hat, topstitch.

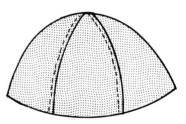

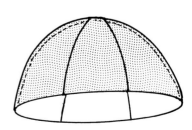

Fig. 2–11

② With right sides together, sew long sides of chin straps closed and turn right side out. With right sides together, sew one cap to the brim. Attach chin straps between lining and hat, or sew chin straps in place. Sew lining in place by machine or hand (Fig. 2–12).

Fig. 2–13

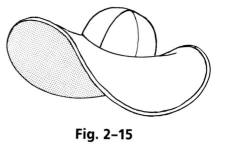

Fig. 2–15

④ Sew bias tape to wrong side by hand or machine, leaving an opening for the boning (Fig. 2–14).

Case

❶ Find the center of your gusset and cut a line 11 inches (27.5cm) angling out at the ends like an envelope (Fig. 2–16).

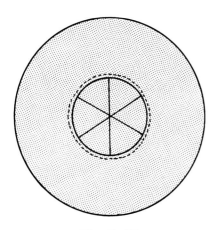

Fig. 2–12

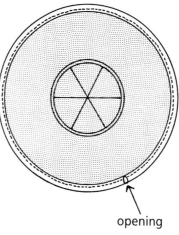

opening

Fig. 2–14

Fig. 2–16

❷ Baste and sew zipper in place, turning raw edges of opening toward wrong side (Fig. 2–17).

Fig. 2–17

❸ The purpose of the bias tape is to form an exterior casing for the boning. Iron one long edge of the bias tape ¼ inch (6mm) toward the wrong side. With right sides together, sew the unpressed edge of the bias tape to outer brim edge, folding the beginning of the bias tape ¼ inch (6mm) back (Fig. 2–13).

❺ Sew boning together so that it is double thickness. Insert the double boning through the opening in the bias tape. Push in as much as possible, making the brim tight (Fig. 2–15). Sew ends together and close.

❸ Sew strap on the long side and turn right side out. Press so that seam runs down the center back (Fig. 2–18). Turn raw ends in and pin strap to gusset 1 inch (2.5cm) away from zipper and sew in place (Fig. 2–19). Sew short ends of gusset to form a circle (Fig. 2–20).

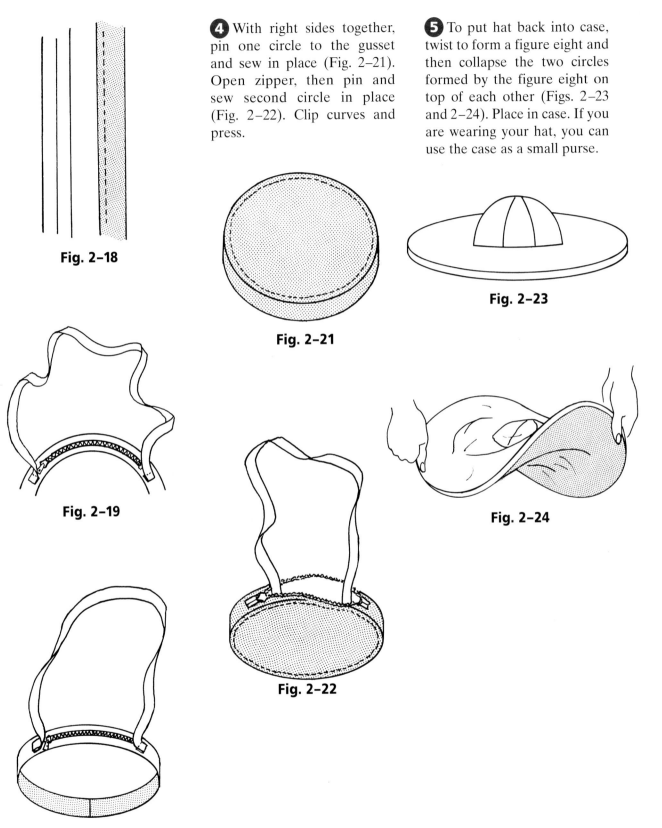

4 With right sides together, pin one circle to the gusset and sew in place (Fig. 2–21). Open zipper, then pin and sew second circle in place (Fig. 2–22). Clip curves and press.

5 To put hat back into case, twist to form a figure eight and then collapse the two circles formed by the figure eight on top of each other (Figs. 2–23 and 2–24). Place in case. If you are wearing your hat, you can use the case as a small purse.

Fig. 2–18

Fig. 2–21

Fig. 2–23

Fig. 2–19

Fig. 2–24

Fig. 2–22

Fig. 2–20

FROM CAP TO SACK OR SACK TO CAP

... EAT YOUR HAT?

Have you ever gone to the park with your kids when they decide to start a rock, leaf, or feather collection, and suddenly you find yourself in charge of it? Well, if you have this nifty hat, you can convert it into a bag and you're set. Also, you can teach your children to do their part for the environment by having them tote their lunch to school in the bag and then wearing the hat home again. Four sizes are available, child through adult.

It's a cap! It's a sack! It's a wearable alternative to paper and plastic bags!

✓ Materials

- ○ ½ yard (45cm) fabric
- ○ ¼ yard (22.5cm) extra-heavy interfacing
- ○ One package of double-fold bias tape
- ○ Scrap piece of ¼-inch-(6mm) wide elastic

Preparation

- Prewash all fabrics.
- Cut 4 brims from the pattern at the back of the book.
- Interface two of the brim sections.
- Cut twelve hat sections from the pattern at the back of the book.

Directions

right side

wrong side

❶ Sew three hat sections right sides together to form a half circle (Fig. 2–25). Repeat, forming three more half circles with the remaining sections.

Fig. 2–25

2 Sew two half circles together to form a circle (Fig. 2–26). Repeat to form a second circle.

Fig. 2–26

3 Sew two brim pieces, one with interfacing, right sides together, leaving an opening for turning (Fig. 2–27). Repeat for the remaining two brim sections.

Fig. 2–27

4 Attach a brim to hat, right sides together, so that the center of the brim hits the center of one of the hat sections (Fig. 2–28). Repeat for second hat.

Fig. 2–28

5 On one of the hats, on the center-back section, sew a

small piece of elastic ⅜ inch (1cm) above the raw edge to the wrong side (Fig. 2-29). Pull on the elastic while sewing so that it will gather the hat in.

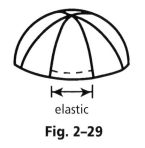

elastic

Fig. 2–29

6 Take the two hats you have sewn and place them right sides together. Sew them together along the lower edge, leaving the brim as an opening. Backstitch at start and finish (Fig. 2-30).

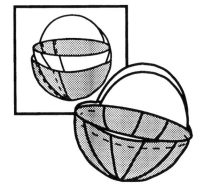

Fig. 2–30

7 Form a strap for the bag by using double bias tape. Start by sewing the fold of the tape to the raw edge at the center back of the hat. (You are using the bias tape to hide the raw edges of the hat and then it becomes the strap.) When you reach the brim, sew through the bias tape only, creating the strap. Continue sewing the

bias tape to the hat on the other side of the brim, and stop at the center back. Make strap length (from brim to brim) approximately 40 inches (1m) long (Fig. 2–31).

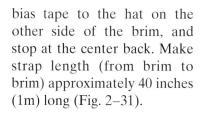

Fig. 2–31

8 To wear the hat, fold one hat into the other, wrong sides together, with the straps hidden inside (Fig. 2–32).

Fig. 2–32

9 To convert the hat to a bag, pull the brims open and pull out the straps. Fill the bag and fold the brims over to close it (Fig. 2–33).

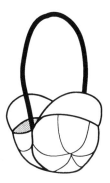

Fig. 2–33

SUNGLASS VISOR

Sometimes you don't want the burden of a hat, or maybe hats make you too hot. However, you still want that extra protection for your face, or perhaps you don't have prescription sunglasses. The Sunglass Visor is the perfect solution. It snaps onto the handles of your glasses. This no-sew item can be made out of the leftovers from the Flat Hat (see pages 12–13).

Follow the fabric preparation according to the instructions for the Flat Hat. Cut out one Sunglass Visor from the pattern at the back of the book. Install an O-ring type pronged snap at the dots on either side of the visor. Snap it around your glasses. You can also add optional bias tape around the outer edges as was done on the Bandanna Visor if you prefer a more finished edge.

inches (30 × 30cm), adult = 13 × 13 inches (32.5 × 32.5cm). Fold the square in half horizontally. Place the negative triangle template on one side of the square, matching the fold and a straight edge. Cut away the triangle. Repeat for the other side. You should now have an hourglass shape (Fig. 2–34).

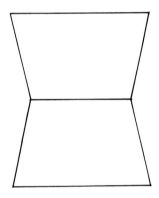

Fig. 2–34

SKI CAP

This snugly warm hat made from polar fleece goes together in no time, and I promise no cold ears or neck! Included are three sizes because every member of your family will want one. Just start with a basic square, and then use the negative template to achieve the right shape. A purchased shoelace makes the best tie.

✓Materials

- ❍ ½ yard (45cm) polar fleece (This makes one adult and one child hat.)
- ❍ One shoelace 36 to 45 inches (90 to 112.5cm) long

Preparation

- • Cut two band sections.
- • Cut the appropriate size square for the crown: baby = 10½ × 10½ inches (26.25 × 26.25cm), child = 12 × 12

Directions

1 Fold crown in, half right sides together, and seam the sides using a ¼ inch (6mm) seam (Fig. 2–35).

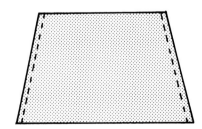

Fig. 2–35

2 Pinch the two upper corners together and sew together, creating a ¼ inch (6mm) seam. This gives the cap its sporty tuck at the top (Fig. 2–36).

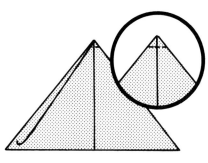

Fig. 2–36

3 Attach shoelaces or drawstring to the right side of one of the band sections at the notches (Fig. 2–37). Close both band sections (Fig. 2–38).

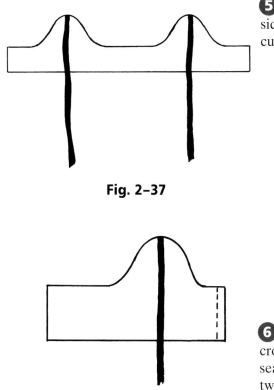

Fig. 2–37

Fig. 2–38

4 Place the band sections right sides together, and tuck the laces on the inside. Sew around the curved sides, double stitching at the straps (Fig. 2–39).

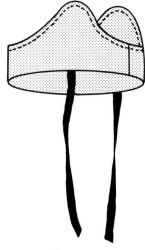

Fig. 2–39

5 Turn band section right side out, and topstitch around curved edge (Fig. 2–40).

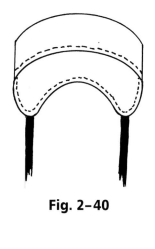

Fig. 2–40

6 Attach the band to the crown, using a ½ inch (12mm) seam allowance. Trim the inner two layers of seam allowance back to ¼ inch (6mm), leaving

½ inch (12mm) on the outside (Fig. 2–41).

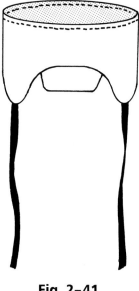

Fig. 2–41

7 Topstitch around the crown, catching the ½-inch (12mm) seam allowance, which will conceal the others (Fig. 2–42).

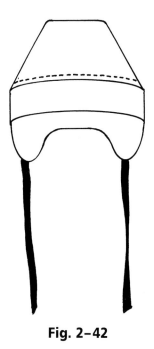

Fig. 2–42

CHAPTER 3

GETTING THERE

CLOTHES

Making Wise Fabric Choices

Some excellent new fabrics as well as old favorites are exceptionally good for travel. Each one has special properties to look for depending on what time of the year it is and where you are heading.

Supplex: A water-repellent lightweight nylon that dries quickly, so it's great for washing when you're on the go. It is used frequently in sportswear such as jogging suits, shorts, swim trunks, and reversible jackets. It is also easy to sew with and can be rolled up into a small pouch and popped back out with almost no wrinkles.

Ultrex: A new high-tech fabric that is 100% waterproof but allows your sweat vapors to escape through tiny micropores. It's not stiff like conventional raincoat fabrics. Its seams require sealing in order to be completely waterproof, however. This fabric is excellent for rain and snow gear as well as for waterproof accessories. Unlike Supplex, garments made of this fabric can't be rolled up into a pouch because it causes wrinkles; also, this fabric doesn't compress well. The wrong side of the fabric tends to cling to the sewing machine, so you should use a Teflon foot, roller foot, or walking foot to help transport it along. The finished product is well worth any frustration.

Rip-stop Nylon: Looks and feels like Supplex but can easily be distinguished because of the little squares visible in the weave. Strong nylon threads are woven into the fabric vertically and horizontally, usually in $1/4$-inch (6mm) intervals, making this a very durable fabric. It is excellent for pouches and drawstring sacks because of its strength and is also easy to sew with.

Fabu-Leather: A man-made leather that is every bit as luxurious as the real thing, if not better. It's slightly stretchy and recovers well, making it perfect for travel. The inside has a tricot lining that adds to the comfort factor. Best of all, you can toss it in the washer and dryer. From swing coats to bikinis, there is no limit to what you can sew with it. Use a sharp needle and a glue stick for basting. Don't let the cost of this fine fabric scare you away. I guarantee that an outfit made with Fabu-Leather will be your favorite.

Silk: A continuous protein filament secreted by the silkworm and used to form a cocoon. Silk is exceptionally popular in tropical climates because it holds up to 30% of its weight in moisture, and it is mildew-resistant. It also has excellent insulating properties when used as a filling in garments, which means you achieve maximum warmth for minimum weight. Although some silks require dry-cleaning, many types can be washed by hand. Sew with a very fine, sharp needle and polyester thread.

Ramie: An Asian plant with high moisture absorption and high drying capabilities. By itself it's usually used for fishing nets and hats. Most of the time you will find it blended with cotton. It doesn't have a good stretch recovery but is mildew-resistant.

Rayon: A man-made textile fiber produced from cellulose (wood). Rayon holds 13% of its weight in moisture. It has very low elasticity but excellent draping qualities. Dry-cleaning is commonly recommended because harsh detergents destruct the fibers. Some varieties can be hand washed in a mild detergent and hung to dry.

Terry Toweling: Best when made from 100% cotton. It absorbs well but because of the weight and thickness, it takes long to dry. It is wonderfully warm to wrap yourself in when coming out of the water. Serge raw edges first and use a ball point needle when sewing. Or you can make fell seams.

Iron-on Vinyl: Available in different widths and finishes such as shiny or matte. There are a variety of different types on the market. Pay special attention to the recommended iron settings and washing instructions. Make sure all fabric has been washed and ironed first. Take care to clip any threads so that they don't get fused in.

MAKING WISE PATTERN CHOICES

Whether you're traveling by horseback or airplane, chances are you'll be sitting to get to your destination. Of course, pants or shorts are the number one choice on most people's list. But even your favorite jeans might start to hurt or pinch after a few hours. Seams you never knew existed suddenly cause you to squirm all over your seat. (Please remember that this also applies to children.) So, when you select a pants pattern (many of these tips apply to skirts too), try to avoid the following:

A lot of topstitching

Bulky side pockets

Tightness around the thighs

Short crotch seams

Rear zippers

Rear pockets

Tight waists

Also avoid stiff fabrics and fabrics that might bag out at the knees. A 100% cotton knit won't travel as well as one with 8 to 10% Lycra in it. Look for the following when you make your pants (or skirt) selections.

Elastic pull-on waists, possibly with an adjustable cord

Lower crotch seams for sitting comfort

Simple flat seams

Front panel pockets

It would be nice if comfort always ranked first, but, unfortunately, there are times when we have to look our best. Sometimes you can compromise on long trips by wearing something comfortable and then slipping into a change of clothing just before arrival. If that isn't possible, then sometimes wearing an outfit made from a simple pattern and a more luxurious fabric can do the trick too. One of my favorites for this purpose is Fabu-Leather. Not only will you look chic and feel comfortable, but you will be practical. Spills wipe off, the fabric won't bag, and you can throw it in the washer and dryer.

It's always a good idea to have a travel coat—something that's not too heavy and isn't sensitive to being stuffed into an overhead bin or car trunk. Classics such as swing coats and trench coats fit the bill. If your destination is less glamorous, try a poncho or cape.

DRAPE TRICKS

If you're really daring and plan on spending a few days in a tropical environment where you'll be by the water most of the time, try sewing one or two multipurpose drapes. They require very little space, time, or talent. Throw into your bag a few bathing suits and a pair of shorts and you're set. You'll be the height of fashion with no luggage!

Select lightweight, drapey fabrics such as a rayon challis. With any luck you will find them 60 inches (150cm) wide. (For nicer twists and ties, 60-inch fabric works better.) Just hem all four sides. You can also run a zigzag stitch 1 inch (2.5cm) in from the edges and then pull the threads to create a fringe.

Fig. 3–2

SMALL DRAPE
(45 x 45 inches [112.5 x 112.5cm])

TRICK 1. BAG OR BACKPACK

Fold the drape in half to form a rectangle and tie the corners together (Figs. 3–1 and 3–2). Slip your arms through the openings and wear it on your back. It is perfect for carrying sunscreen, reading material, and other beach items (Fig. 3–3).

Fig. 3–1

MEDIUM DRAPE
(56 x 56 inches [140 x 140cm])

TRICK 2. TOP

Fold the drape in half diagonally to form a triangle. Fold the long side over again approximately 5 inches (12.5cm). Wrap the drape across your bust and crisscross the ties in the back (Fig. 3–4).

Bring the ties to the front and tie them at hip or waist height on the side. This top looks great with shorts (Fig. 3–5).

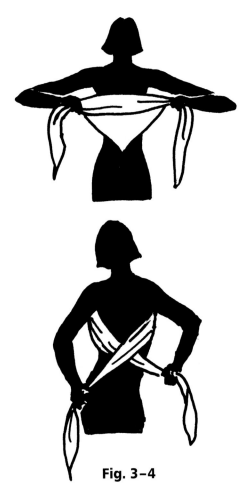

Fig. 3–3

Fig. 3–4

Fig. 3–5

Fig. 3–6

Fig. 3–7

Fig. 3–8

LARGE DRAPE
(2 yards x 45 inches [180 x 112.5cm])

Trick 3. Miniskirt

Fold the drape in half lengthwise so that it is double. Hold the drape behind you and wrap it to the front (Fig. 3–6). Cross and twist the ties. Tuck the twisted ends under the top edge (Fig. 3–7). Secure with a safety pin if desired. This is the perfect thing to wear over your bathing suit, and it's even suitable for lunching at restaurants (Fig. 3–8).

Trick 4. Long Skirt

Tie the drape the same as you did for the miniskirt in Trick 3, but don't double it. After tying the knot, leave the ends out (Fig. 3–9) or tuck them in (Fig. 3–10).

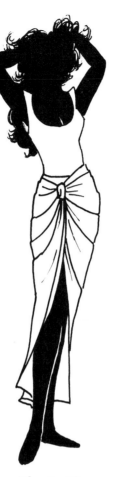

Fig. 3–10

Trick 5. Pant Skirt

From behind, wrap the drape around your left leg, and with your right hand hold the end tight. With your right hand, wrap the other end across the front and around the back, ending where you started. Tie the ends securely together. This is very appealing for evening wear (Fig. 3–11).

Fig. 3–11

Fig. 3–9

Trick 6. Draped Dress

Hold the drape behind you and wrap it around to the front. Cross and twist the ties around your bust. This gives the dress a draped look. Pull the ends tight and twist them as straps to tie behind your neck (Figs. 3–12 and 3–13).

Fig. 3–13

Fig. 3–12

TIP

Printed fabrics show fewer wrinkles and less dirt.

CHAPTER 4

TRAVEL EQUIPMENT

INFANT EQUIPMENT

Traveling with infant equipment on airlines can be very cumbersome. Strollers and car seats can become damaged or dirty. One simple solution is to make a few drawstring bags made from rip-stop nylon and put your equipment into the bag. When you arrive at your destination, you can roll the bag up into virtually nothing and stash it until you need it again.

STROLLER BAG

To measure, collapse your stroller and place your tape measure around its widest spot (this might be by the wheels) to get a circumference. Add 6 inches (15cm). This is the total width of your bag. For the bag length, do the same—measure the stroller's length and add 6 inches (15cm) (Fig. 4-1).

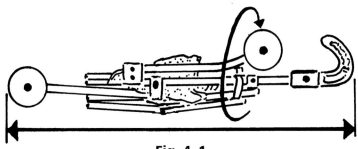

Fig. 4-1

✓Materials

- ❍ Rip-stop nylon to cover stroller dimensions plus an extra ¹/₂ yard (45cm) for the pockets
- ❍ Interfacing
- ❍ 2 yards (180cm) drawstring
- ❍ Two to three reversible snaps
- ❍ Two grommets (optional)

Preparation

- ● Cut the bag from the rip-stop nylon, using the above directions.
- ● Cut two pocket pieces 9 × 8 inches (22.5 × 20cm) so that when you are not using the bag, you can condense it by turning it inside out into the pocket.
- ● Cut one pocket flap 9 × 4 inches (22.5 × 10cm).

Directions

❶ Sew around pocket pieces, right sides together, leaving an opening on one of the longer sides for turning. Turn and press. Topstitch across the pocket top, closing the opening (Fig. 4-2).

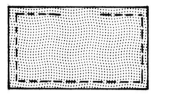

Fig. 4–2

❷ Fold flap in half the long way with right sides together. Sew, leaving an opening on the short end. Turn and press, concealing the raw edges of the opening. Topstitch around three sides, leaving the folded edge (Fig. 4–3).

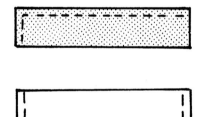

Fig. 4–3

❸ Sew the pocket, centered horizontally, on one-half of bag. Place the flap directly above the pocket, and topstitch it in place along the top edge (Fig. 4–4). Set two to three reversible snaps to close the flap.

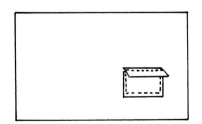

Fig. 4–4

❹ On the upper raw edge of the bag piece on the inside, iron a piece of interfacing 2×2 inches (5×5cm) directly above the pocket (Fig. 4–5). On the interfacing, make two buttonholes or set two grommets $1/2$ inch (12mm) apart and $1 3/4$ inches (4.37cm) down from the upper edge.

❺ Fold bag in half, right sides together, and sew down the side and across the bottom (Fig. 4–6).

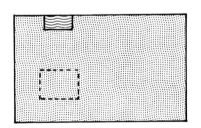

Fig. 4–5

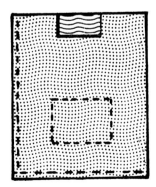

Fig. 4–6

❻ Turn the top raw edge under $1/2$ inch (12mm) and then $1/2$ inch (12mm) again to form a casing for a drawstring. The buttonholes or grommets should be in the center front of your casing. Edgestitch casing in place (Fig. 4–7).

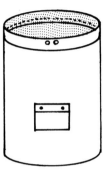

Fig. 4–7

❼ Insert drawstring cord through buttonholes or grommets with a safety pin (Fig. 4–8). When you pack your stroller, make sure your drawstrings get tucked inside the bag. When the stroller bag is not in use, turn it inside out into the pocket on the front of the bag by putting your hand in the pocket and pushing the bag through the bottom inside out.

Fig. 4–8

CAR SEAT BAG

Take measurements for the Car Seat Bag as you did for the Stroller Bag, making sure to measure the circumference at the widest point. Sew, using the same technique as for the Stroller Bag. With the leftover material you can make a few more bags for things such as dirty laundry, shoes, and luggage carts.

BACKPACKS

No travel wardrobe is complete without a matching backpack. Backpacks free up your hands and hold all kinds of things. They are easy to sew, and you can make one out of just about anything. From laminated fabrics to woven rugs, let your imagination run. Included below is a Mini Backpack as a purse alternative. It has a strap that zips together to function as a shoulder strap. When it's unzipped, you can wear it on your back (Fig. 4–9).

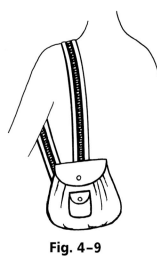

Fig. 4–9

STANDARD-SIZE BACKPACK

✓Materials

○ 1¼ yards (112.5cm) of fabric

○ ½ yard (45cm) of interfacing

○ Two large grommets

○ Pair of parachute clips 1 to 1½ inches (2.5 to 3.75cm) wide

○ Two yards (1.8m) of 1-inch- (2.5cm) wide nylon webbing for no-sew straps (optional)

Preparation

● For the backpack sack, cut a rectangle 18 × 30 inches (30 × 75cm).

● Cut two straps 3½ × 40 inches (8.75 x 100cm).

● Cut one drawstring 1½ inches × 44 inches (3.75 × 110cm).

● Cut four pocket flaps and two backpack sack flaps on the fold using the patterns at the back of the book.

● Cut two pockets from the pattern at the back of the book. Mark the pleats.

Directions

1 Interface two pocket flaps and one backpack flap. With right sides together, sew the two pocket flaps and the sack flap, leaving an opening between dots (Fig. 4–10). Clip curves, turn, and press. Topstitch around the curved edge only (Fig. 4–11).

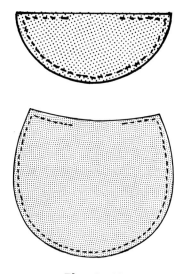

Fig. 4–10

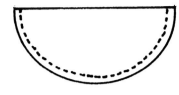

Fig. 4–11

2 On pocket pieces, turn and press raw edges on sides and bottom ¼ inch (6mm) toward the wrong side. On the top edge turn and press ¼ inch (6mm) and then ¼ inch (6mm) again (Fig. 4–12). Stitch across the top edge (Fig. 4–13).

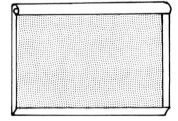

Fig. 4–12

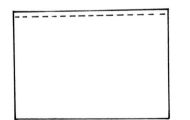

Fig. 4–13

3 Pin pockets to the sack piece 1½ inches (3.75cm) to either side of center and 2½ inches (6.25cm) from the bottom. Form the pleat in the pocket. The finished pocket width should be 5½ inches (13.75cm)

wide after pleating. Stitch the sides in place first, taking care not to catch the pleat (Fig. 4–14). Then sew across the bottom, this time catching the pleat (Fig. 4–15).

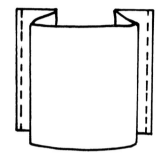

Fig. 4–14

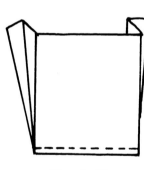

Fig. 4–15

4 Place the pocket flaps ½ inch (12mm) above the pockets. Sew across the flap, closing the opening of the flap at the same time (Fig. 4–16).

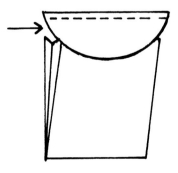

Fig. 4–16

5 Close the center-back seam of the backpack sack piece. Turn and press the top edge under ¼ inch (6mm) and then 1¼ inches (3.1cm) to form a drawstring casing (Fig. 4–17). Don't sew yet.

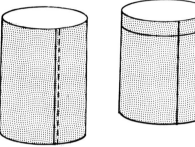

Fig. 4–17

6 Place two grommets ½ inch (6mm) apart and 2 inches (5cm) to each side of center from the unfolded, pressed top raw edge through one layer of fabric only. When casing is folded down, grommets should be in the center of the casing (Fig. 4–18). *Do not sew casing yet.*

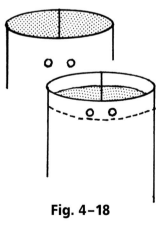

Fig. 4–18

7 Sew straps, turn, and press with seam down the center back (Fig. 4–19).

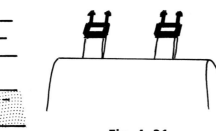

Fig. 4–19

8 Position pack flap on the outside center back even with the lower edge of the casing. Tuck straps under the flap 1/4 inch (6mm) to each side of center (Fig. 4–20). Sew casing catching flap and straps at the same time. Backstitch at start and finish.

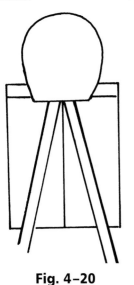

Fig. 4–20

9 Cut an 8-inch (20cm) piece off each strap. Slip the lower buckle portion onto the short straps and fold them in half (Fig. 4–21). Pin them 1 1/2 inches (3.75cm) in from the outer edge of the pack with the

buckle facing the outside of the bag. From the wrong side you can just see the strap ends.

Fig. 4–21

10 Turn the pack wrong side out and sew across the bottom, catching the straps (Fig. 4–22). Backstitch at each strap for extra reinforcement.

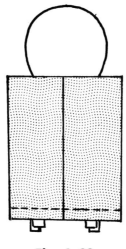

Fig. 4–22

11 From the wrong side, sew across the bottom of the pack corners, forming triangles to square off the bag (Fig. 4–23).

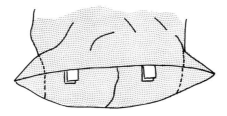

Fig. 4–23

12 Sew the drawstring with a 1/4-inch (6mm) seam allowance and then trim it back to 1/8 inch (3mm). Turn and insert through grommets and casing. Tie knots on the ends (Fig. 4–24).

Fig. 4–24

13 Attach upper buckle portion to longer straps and thread so that straps are adjustable (Fig. 4–25).

Fig. 4–25

Top: This standard size backpack can be made to match your travel wardrobe.

Bottom: The straps on the mini backpack can be zipped together for use as a shoulder bag.

2 For the straps, sew right sides together 1 inch (2.5cm) at the top and 1 inch (2.5cm) at the bottom along the long side. Turn right side out and sandwich one-half of the zipper in each of the long seams (Fig. 4–27).

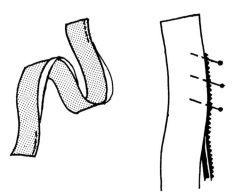

Fig. 4–27

Mini Backpack

✓ Materials

❍ ¾ yard (68cm) of fabric

❍ ½ yard (45cm) of interfacing

❍ 28-to-30-inch (70 to 73cm) separating zipper

❍ Two large grommets

Preparation

● Cut one backpack sack rectangle 14 × 25 inches (35 x 62.5cm).

● Cut two straps 3 × 32 inches (7.5 x 80cm).

● Cut one drawstring 1½ × 34 inches (3.75 × 85cm).

● Cut two pocket flaps and two sack flaps.

● Cut one pocket 8 × 6½ inches (20 × 16.25cm).

● Interface straps, flaps, and 2½ inches (6.2cm) down across the top edge on the sack.

Directions

1 Sew together the same as you did the Standard-Size Backpack except for the pocket, which should be sewn to the center of the sack rectangle (Fig. 4–26).

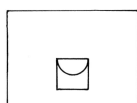

Fig. 4–26

3 Zip the strap together and sew the strap in the pack at the center top and bottom. You can wear your pack two ways: Zipped together it will form one solid shoulder strap so that you can wear it as a purse; unzipped you can wear it as a backpack (Fig. 4–28).

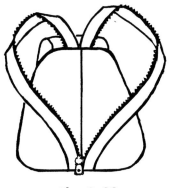

Fig. 4–28

EYEGLASS CASE

If you wear prescription glasses, then you will want to carry a spare pair on your trip. Sunglasses are a must and should be packed as well. Here is a pattern for an extra case. If you dig deep enough in your scrap box, you can probably find all the materials necessary, or just use leftovers from some of the projects in this book.

✓Materials

- ❑ 27 inches (67.5cm) of double-fold, narrow bias tape (Folded it is ¼ inch [6mm] wide; or make your own.)
- ❑ ¼ yard (22.5cm) of fabric or leftovers to fit the pattern pieces
- ❑ Velcro or snap closure
- ❑ Batting or interfacing (optional) (If you cushion the case with batting, add an extra ¼ inch [6mm] seam allowance. Laminate or iron heavy interfacing to stiffen it.)

Directions

1 Using the patterns from the back of the book, cut two fronts and two backs. If using Velcro, sew a square to the inside section of the back and to the outside of the front where indicated on the patterns (Fig. 4–29).

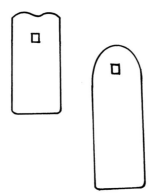

Fig. 4–29

2 Sandwich interfacing or batting between wrong sides of the pieces, or laminate half the pieces from the right side (Fig. 4–30).

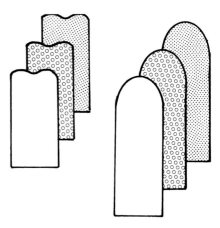

Fig. 4–30

3 With all the right sides facing outward and the wrong sides together, sandwich double-folded bias tape across the top of the front section. Stitch in place. Place front section on top of back section and pin edges even (Fig. 4–31).

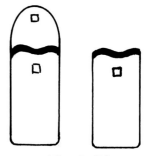

Fig. 4–31

4 From the front side, pin sandwiched bias tape all around the outside of case, starting and ending at the center bottom. Sew bias tape in place (Fig. 4–32).

Fig. 4–32

INSULATED BOTTLE CARRIERS

5 Add snap if necessary (Fig. 4–33).

Fig. 4–33

The best way to avoid dehydration is to carry a water bottle with you. Perfect for plane and car rides, water bottles can also be taken to the park or pool. Make an insulated bottle holder to help keep things warm or cold. When you add a strap, you can carry it anywhere. Bottle holders also make nice gift packaging for wine bottles. You will find two different patterns, one for a wine bottle and one for a 9-ounce (0.5L) personal water bottle (this size can also hold a baby bottle).

TIP

A few days before departure get a bin or basket and put it in a centrally located area. Start putting in it the items you see around the house that you know you will want to pack, such as sunglasses, spare key, lotion, etc. This will help reduce stress in the heat of packing.

These insulated bottle bags can be used for wine, water, or baby bottles. Handles and straps can be made out of cording and webbing.

✓Materials

- ❍ ½ yard (45cm) of 45-inch-(112.5cm) wide fabric
- ❍ ⅓ yard (30cm) of quilt batting, Thinsulite, or foam rubber for insulation
- ❍ 12 inches (30cm) of draw-string cording
- ❍ 38 inches (95cm) of draw-string cording (optional)

Preparation

- Cut three bottle bottoms from the pattern at the back of the book, two of fabric, and one of insulation.

- Cut three bottle sides, two of fabric and one of insulation. Wine bottle: 12½ × 9 inches (31.25 × 22.5cm); water bottle: 10½ × 6½ inches (26.25 × 16.25cm).

- Cut one drawstring top from the fabric. Wine bottle: 12½ × 4½ inches (31.25 × 11.25cm); water bottle: 10½ × 3¼ inches (26.25 × 8cm).

Directions

❶ Baste insulation to the wrong side of one bottle bottom and one bottle side (Fig. 4–34).

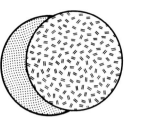
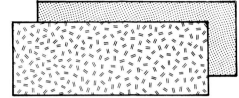

Fig. 4–34

❷ With right sides together, close the sides of the insulated bottle side as well as the other bottle side (Fig. 4–35).

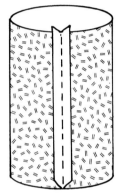

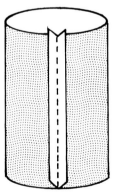

Fig. 4–35

❸ With right sides together, sew the insulated bottom to the insulated side (Fig. 4–36). Repeat for uninsulated pieces. This will be the liner.

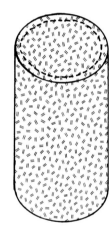

Fig. 4–36

❹ Close the side seams of the drawstring top piece by sewing down 1 inch (2.5cm). Then leave a ½-inch (12mm) opening. Finish closing the side, backstitching at both start and finish (Fig. 4–37).

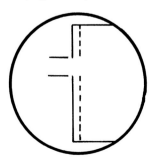

Fig. 4–37

5 Hem the upper edge for the drawstring casing by folding down ¹/₂ inch (12mm) and then ¹/₂ inch (12mm) again toward the wrong side. The opening should now line up with the center front of the casing. Topstitch casing in place (Fig. 4–38).

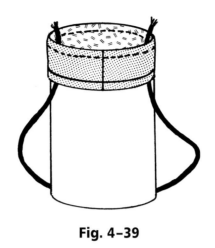

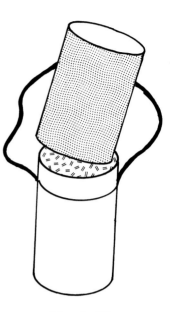

Fig. 4–39

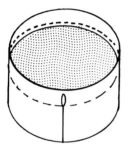

Fig. 4–38

6 With right sides together and raw edges even, attach the drawstring top piece to the insulated bottle piece (Fig. 4–39). Optional: If you wish to have shoulder straps on your bottle carrier, sew them in place now. A good length is 38 inches (95cm). You can braid or make your own cord as shown on pages 61–62 in Chapter 5. Place them on either side of the side seams, and sew them in place when you attach the drawstring to the piece.

7 Place the bottle lining inside the insulated piece with wrong sides together (Fig. 4–40). Turn the top raw edge of the liner to the wrong side and stitch in place by hand or machine. Make sure your strap ends are tucked in (Fig. 4–41).

8 Insert drawstring.

Fig. 4–40

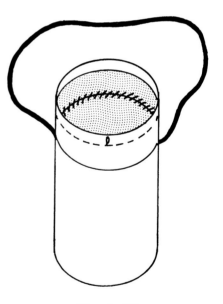

Fig. 4–41

FANNY PACKS

Have you ever found yourself at the zoo or on a hike and suddenly you are carrying four jackets, even though you left with just one? "Good old Mom" becomes a human clothes rack again. You can avoid this problem by sewing exterior pockets to nylon windbreakers and ponchos that convert to fanny packs. If the weather is questionable, you can buckle the pack around your waist leaving your hands free. When you need a jacket, you can pull it out; if you're too hot, take it off and roll it up. There are commercially available patterns for jackets such as these, but you can sew a pocket to your own favorite windbreaker or jacket. Patterns at the back of the book are in 3 sizes: S, M, L. Note: This concept is suitable only for garments made of Supplex or Nylon, material that can be wadded up into a ball without wrinkling.

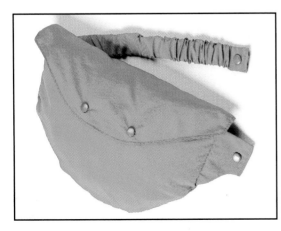

This fanny pack can also be sewn onto a rain poncho (Chapter 4). The poncho can then be folded into the pack and worn on the hip.

✓ Materials

- ❍ ½ yard (45cm) of Supplex
- ❍ 1-inch- (2.5cm) wide non-roll elastic
- ❍ Three reversible snaps

Preparation

- ● Cut one strap from Supplex 3 inches wide (7.5cm) by 13 inches (32.5cm) for small; 15 inches (37.5cm) for medium; and 19 inches (47.5cm) for large.
- ● Cut one piece of elastic (small, 8 inches [20cm]; medium, 10 inches [25cm]; large, 13 inches [32.5cm]).
- ● Cut two fanny packs on fold.
- ● Cut two fanny pack flaps on fold.
- ● Cut two strap extensions on fold from the pattern at the back of the book.

Directions

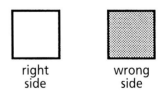

right side   wrong side

❶ With right sides together, sew around fanny pack and fanny pack flap, leaving an opening between dots. Clip corners and curves, turn, and press (Fig. 4–42).

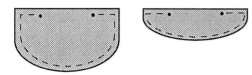

Fig. 4-42

2 Topstitch across sides and lower curved edge of flap and across the top of the pack only (Fig. 4-43).

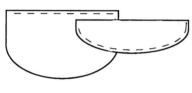

Fig. 4-43

3 With right sides together, close long side of strap (Fig. 4-44). Turn right side out and insert elastic, securing with stitches on one end. On the other end, turn raw edge in ¹/₄ inch (6mm) and stitch opening closed, securing elastic at the same time. Smooth gathers away and stitch 1 inch (2.5cm) in from the end through the elastic again (Figs. 4-45 and 4-46). This is where a snap will go.

Fig. 4-44

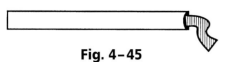

Fig. 4-45

Fig. 4-46

4 Fold one strap extension right sides together on fold line. Sew across the top and bottom, turn, and press (Fig. 4-47). On the smaller side, press raw edges toward the inside ¹/₄ inch (6mm). Repeat with the remaining strap extension. With right sides together, baste the folded sides of the strap extensions to the fanny pack edges (Fig. 4-48).

Fig. 4-47

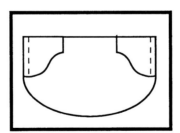

Fig. 4-48

5 Place fanny pack on back or front of garment with the strap extensions *face down* on the garment. Sew fanny pack in place, backstitching at start and finish.

6 Place flap just above pack, and sew across the straight edge, backstitching at both ends and closing the opening on the flap at the same time (Fig. 4-49).

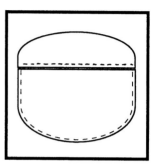

Fig. 4-49

Fold flap down and topstitch across the top of the flap again (Fig. 4-50).

Fig. 4-50

7 Edgestitch left strap extension closed. On the right side, insert elastic strap with the unfinished edge into the strap extension opening. Sew in place. Note: This illustration shows the pocket from the inside! Install snaps as shown (Fig. 4-51).

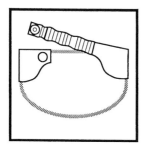

Fig. 4–51

8 To get the jacket in the waist pack: Roll it up as small as possible and then turn it inside out through the bottom of the pocket. Install snaps on pouch with the jacket on the inside.

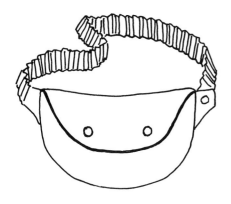

RAIN PONCHO

Using 60-inch- (150cm) wide Supplex, you can construct a simple but functional rain poncho that snaps down the side. The fanny pack described above can be sewn to the front or back so that the poncho can be folded into the pack. The pattern for the hood for the Beach Towel Cover-Up in Chapter 5 fits this poncho. Try using contrasting colors for the hood and fanny pack. Because the poncho is constructed from a rectangle you can choose the length best for you.

✓Materials

❍ Nylon or Supplex twice the length of the poncho plus ½ yard (45cm) for hood

❍ Interfacing

❍ 1 yard of drawstring cording

❍ Two grommets

❍ Twelve reversible snaps

❍ 7-inch plastic #5 YKK zipper or equivalent plastic zipper

Preparation

● Cut a piece of 60-inch- (150cm) wide fabric the length you want your poncho to be. This measurement should reflect the front length as well as the back. Check the width (your arm span) and, if necessary, trim it.

● Cut four hoods from the pattern at the back of the book and a zipper placket, one fabric and one interfacing.

Directions

1 For snap reinforcement, iron a 1-inch- (2.5cm) wide strip of interfacing along the whole length of the two long sides of the poncho (Fig. 4–52). Position interfacing ¼ inch (6mm) in from the raw edge. Hem all around the poncho by pressing the long sides, first ¼ inch (6mm) and then 1 inch (2.5cm), toward the wrong side. Across the bottom (the shorter sides) turn up ½ inch (12mm) and then ½ inch (12mm) again. Edgestitch all around the poncho (Fig. 4–53).

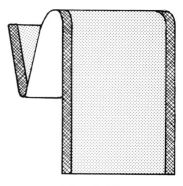

Fig. 4–52

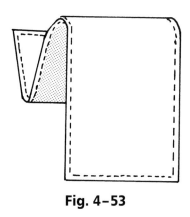

Fig. 4-53

2 To cut the neck hole, fold the poncho in fourths, first horizontally and then vertically. Place the neck negative template from the back of the book in the upper folded corner. Cut the neck out (Fig. 4–54). Staystitch around the hole.

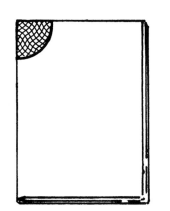

Fig. 4-54

3 Iron interfacing to zipper placket and finish raw edges. Place it under the neck opening on the center front of the poncho, right sides to-

gether (Fig. 4–55). Sew along dotted lines, then cut along solid line down the center and into the corners like an envelope. Be careful not to cut through the stitching! Turn and press facing to the wrong side.

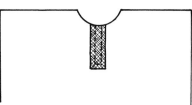

Fig. 4-55

4 Baste zipper in opening and sew in place (Fig. 4–56).

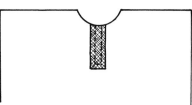

Fig. 4-56

5 Sew hood pieces together along center back. Repeat for lining. Reinforce grommet area with a square of interfacing on outer hood only. Install grommets on outer hood only. Place hood lining in hood, right sides together, and sew around front edge. Turn right side out (Fig. 4–57).

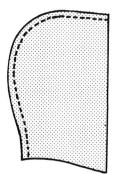

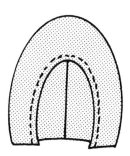

Fig. 4-57

6 Sew outer hood to poncho, matching center backs and keeping lining free. Turn raw edge of lining under ¼ inch (6mm), and edgestitch to poncho (Fig. 4–58).

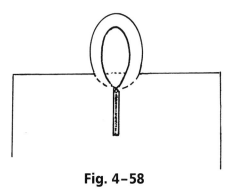

Fig. 4-58

7 To create drawstring casing, stitch along the hood front approximately 1 inch (2.5cm) in from the hood edge (grommet should be in the center of the casing). Insert drawstring (Fig. 4–59).

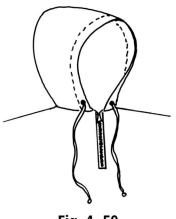

Fig. 4–59

8 To install the snaps, start 3 inches up from the bottom of the sides, placing six snaps 5 inches apart per side so that the poncho overlaps to the back (Fig. 4–60).

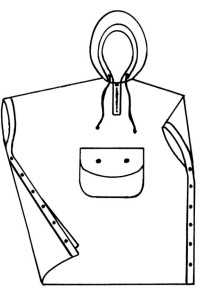

Fig. 4–60

TRAVEL PILLOW THAT CONVERTS TO A REST MAT

I'll never forget the faces of the flight personnel on one of our annual trips to Switzerland to visit my parents when my two children got on board with their travel pillows complete with ID tags. This pillow is perfect for the plane, trips to Grandma's house, exercise class, or nursery school. It features a convenient carrying handle and unfolds to a 19- x 52-inch (48 x 132cm) rest mat. You can sew the optional straps to carry it backpack style.

✓Materials

- ❍ 2¼ yards (2m) of 45-inch- (112.5cm) wide fabric
- ❍ One roll of quilt batting 90 x 108 inches (225 x 270cm)
- ❍ 12-inch (30cm) length of 1-inch- (2.5cm) wide nylon webbing for handle

Directions

1 Make sure top and bottom edges of fabric are straight. With right sides together, stitch across the top and down the long side. Leave the bottom open (Fig. 4–61). Turn right side out and press.

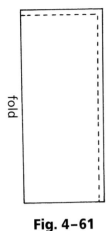

Fig. 4–61

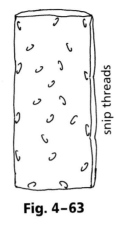

Fig. 4–63

form the pillow. Turn and pin raw edge in ¼ inch (6mm). On one side of pillow, sandwich handle 5 inches (12.5cm) from the top and bottom of the pillow. Pin all around pillow and edges. Topstitch around whole mat, closing bottom opening and pillow sides at the same time (Fig. 4–65).

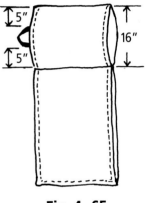

Fig. 4–65

2 Unroll batting from package. It should be the same width as the mat. Push it up into the rest mat making sure it goes all the way to the top and in the corners. Smooth out any lumps and cut it ¼ inch (6mm) shorter than the bottom edge (Fig. 4–62).

4 With a buttonhole stitch, bar tack fifteen to twenty times approximately every 4 inches (10cm) apart. This can be in a random pattern, or you can choose a recurring pattern in your print, for example, on all the blue cars or on the ears, etc. Bar tack back and forth, then simply lift the pressure foot and pull the thread to the next spot. When you're done, snip threads on both sides (Fig. 4–64).

To convert the entire mat into a large pillow, fold the lower edge over twice toward the pillow opening and tuck in (Fig. 4–66).

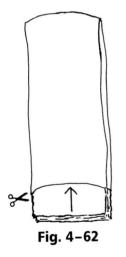

Fig. 4–62

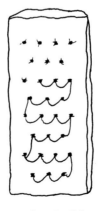

Fig. 4–64

Fig. 4–66

3 Using safety pins, randomly pin through all layers to hold the batting in place (Fig. 4–63).

5 Topstitch across the top edge first before folding top edge over 16 inches (40cm) to

ID Tag

Airlines require that all luggage as well as carry-on items have ID tags. You can sew several of these and attach them to your strollers, suitcases, backpacks, and duffel bags. If you make the tags out of brightly colored fabric, your luggage will be easier to spot. This tag is also the perfect size to slip a business card into. They make great gift tags at Christmas and can, of course, be reused.

❸ Place the two straps wrong sides together, and sew all around. Install a snap at the end (Fig. 4–69).

✓Materials

- ○ Scraps from a nonfraying fabric such as synthetic leather or suede
- ○ Clear plastic or vinyl
- ○ One snap

Fig. 4–67

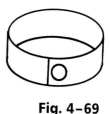

Fig. 4–69

Preparation

- Using the patterns at the back of the book, cut one tag with a window, one without a window, and two straps from the fabric.
- From the plastic, cut one tag and then trim it all around ⅛ inch (3mm) smaller.

❷ Place top tag (with window) and bottom tag (without window) wrong sides together. Sew around outer edges, leaving an opening between dots. Backstitch at start and finish (Fig. 4–68).

❹ Cut a slit through both layers of tag for strap by using the point of your scissors. Insert strap through slit and snap it to close (Fig. 4–70).

Directions

❶ Sew the plastic tag to the tag with a window by placing it under the window and sewing around window opening. Backstitch (Fig. 4–67).

Fig. 4–68

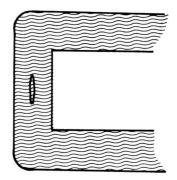

Fig. 4–70

CHAPTER 5

FUN IN THE SUN

SWIMMING POOLS AND BEACHES

Popular family vacation sites usually include swimming pools and beaches. For this chapter I have created a few practical items made from purchased beach towels or bath towels that should make your stay at the beach more pleasant. See Chapter 2 for some easy-to-pack hats. And remember, spending an entire day in the sun can be damaging to your skin. Protect yourself with sufficient sunscreen and wear a beach cover-up and hat.

No-Sew Entertainment

For vacation entertainment, you can create a few no-sew games and even involve your children in the process. This project is suitable for classics such as Checkers, Tic Tac Toe, and Backgammon.

2 Use fabric paint to stencil the game to the solid side of the towel.

3 Use Velcro dots as game pieces. You will find that the hook side of the Velcro sticks better than the loop side. Shells and coins work nicely as game pieces too.

For storing the game pieces, you can sew a pouch directly to the towel. Cut two pouch pieces from the pattern at the back of the book (cotton works best). Sew right sides together, leaving an opening between the dots. Turn, clip corners, and press. Fold up lower edge on fold line to top fold line, and topstitch to towel where desired.

✓Materials

- ○ Bath towel or beach towel with one solid side
- ○ Freezer paper or sheets of Mylar
- ○ Fabric paint
- ○ Black and white Velcro dots

Directions

1 Using the freezer paper or Mylar, cut out a stencil of your favorite game. For this purpose, any type of plastic which you can cut easily will do.

THE ULTIMATE BEACH TOWEL

Throw everything you need into this bag for a trip to the beach except the blanket—it's part of the bag! (Shown with matching case for eyeglasses or sunglasses. See Chapter 4 for instrutions.)

The beach bag/blanket includes an inflatable pillow.

Paradise wouldn't be complete without one of these beach towels. Store-bought towels never seem large enough, so here's one that starts with a regular bath towel and, with the addition of extensions, increases in size. While you are transforming it, add a built-in pillow and secret compartment for money and keys. The whole thing rolls up into a laminated bag that has plenty of room for other things. If you can purchase an inflatable pillow, buy one. Otherwise, the instructions below tell you how to convert kids' water wings into a pillow.

Here are some of the features of this project:

- It converts to a laminated beach bag.
- It has a built-in inflatable pillow.
- It has a secret compartment for money and keys.
- It's enlarged.

TIPS

- Always prewash towels first. They fray a lot when cutting, so be prepared for the mess.

- If you own a serger, use it for finishing the edges only. Sew the seams with a ball point needle. If you do not own a serger, you should make fell seams.

✓Materials

- ○ Bath towel approximately 28 × 50 inches (70 × 125cm). (Note: Towels will vary in size; try to get one as close to this size as possible.)
- ○ 3¼ yards (3m) of coordinating cotton fabric
- ○ Interfacing scraps for valve reinforcement
- ○ 3½ yards (3.15m) of 1-inch-(2.5cm) wide nylon webbing for straps
- ○ One pair of inflatable water wings or an inflatable pillow
- ○ Two to three extra large grommets, depending on how many valves there are on the water wings
- ○ 1¼ yards (1m) of iron-on vinyl
- ○ One 7-inch (18cm) zipper (optional)

Preparation

- From the cotton fabric, cut six bag pieces 19 inches (47.5cm) high by the width of your towel. Cut these all flush to one edge so that you are left with one long continuous piece from which you will cut the side extensions later on.

- With the iron-on vinyl, laminate two of the six bag pieces according to manufacturer's instructions.

- Carefully cut the water wings through a seam to form a flat pillow. You will require two side by side above each other. Try to cut the seams so that the air valves are on the outer edges (Fig. 5–1).

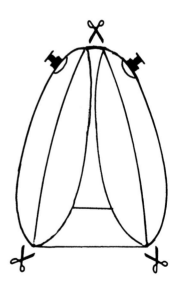

Fig. 5–1

- Cut nylon webbing in half to make two straps.

TIPS

- A drop of sewing machine oil on your needle will help when sewing through the laminated fabric.

- Adjust your stitch one size larger.

LOWER TOWEL EXTENSION

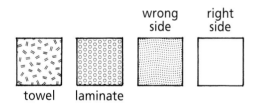

towel   laminate   wrong side   right side

Directions
(All seams ¼ inch [6mm])

1 With a right side and a laminated side together, sew two bag pieces across the top. Turn and press seam with your finger. Topstitch across the top. If your fabric has an obvious direction to it, then turn the unlaminated piece so that the print is going upside down. Repeat with a second bag piece and other laminated piece (Figs. 5–2 and 5–3).

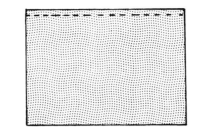

Fig. 5–2

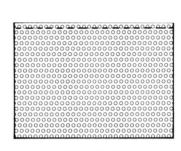

Fig. 5–3

2 On the laminated side of one of the combined bag pieces, with raw edges at the bottom, pin a strap 7 inches (17.5cm) in from each edge. Sew up one side of the strap, across the top, and down the other side, sewing it to the bag piece through both layers. Repeat with second bag piece (Fig. 5–4).

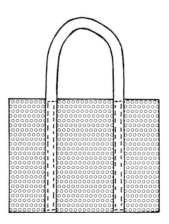

Fig. 5–4

3 Pin the two combined bag pieces to the bottom on each side of the towel, laminated sides out and raw edges even, using a ½-inch (12mm) seam allowance. Trim back to a ¼-inch (6mm) seam allowance (Fig. 5–5).

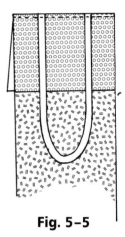

Fig. 5–5

4 Flip the bag sections away from the towel. The laminated sections are now facing each other on the inside. Topstitch across the bag bottom close to the towel edge but not catching the towel. This will conceal the straps. The sides of the bag are still open (Fig. 5–6).

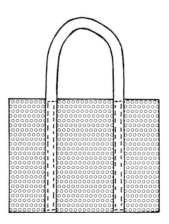

Fig. 5–6

UPPER TOWEL EXTENSION

(This is the pillow portion of your towel. If you wish to skip this part, start with Step 2 and make the pillow casing, and then skip all instructions about the pillow.)

Directions

1 Measure a deflated water wing in length and subtract ¾ inch (1.9cm). This is the new length. Measure the width and multiply by two if you are using water wings (if you are using a pillow, do not multiply by two). Then subtract 1 inch (2.5cm) for your new width. Make a paper pattern using your new length and width (Fig. 5–7).

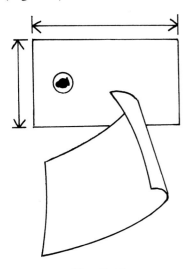

Fig. 5–7

2 To make the pillow casing, sew the remaining two bag sections, right sides together, across the top. Turn and topstitch across the top. Match

center of paper pattern to center of bag, and pin it in place (Fig. 5–8).

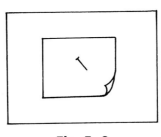

Fig. 5–8

3 Sew around the paper pattern, starting at the bottom 1½ inches (3.75cm) in from the corner and ending on the opposite side 1½ inches (3.75cm) in from the corner. This will leave a large opening at the bottom for inserting the wings or pillow (Fig. 5–9).

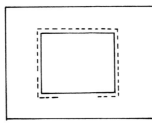

Fig. 5–9

4 Optional: For a larger pillow, you can add another wing to each side going down the long way. Measure the deflated wing in width and subtract ¾ inch (1.9cm). To form another casing, continue sewing from the top across by this new width, then down, matching the height of the existing stitching. Turn the corner with a few stitches and then backstitch (Fig. 5–10).

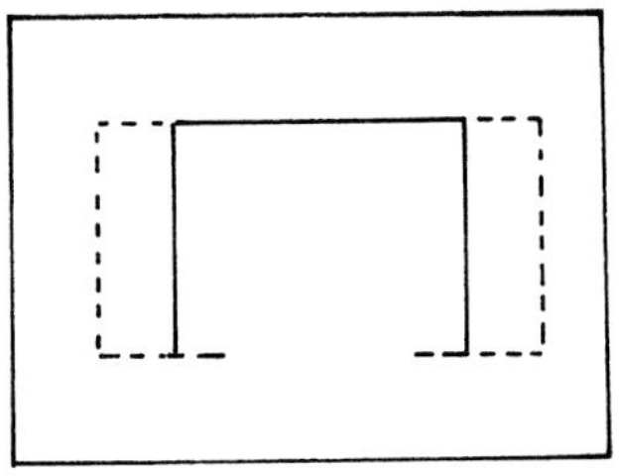

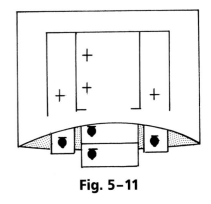

Fig. 5–10

5 Insert and inflate the wings or pillow. Carefully mark the exact valve locations with a pin. Deflate and remove the pillows without disturbing the pins. With a pen, mark all the valve locations from the wrong side (Fig. 5–11).

Fig. 5–11

6 Iron a square of interfacing, a little larger than the grommets, to the inside of the bag at each valve location. For extra reinforcement, on a scrap piece of fabric, iron interfacing and cut squares for each valve (Fig. 5–12). Cut holes for grommets at each valve location as well as each extra reinforced square. Set grommets through pillow casing and squares. Hem the lower edge of the pillow casing on the grommet side only by turning up ¼ inch (6mm) and then ¼ inch (6mm) again (Fig. 5–13).

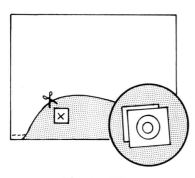

Fig. 5–12

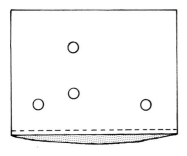

Fig. 5–13

7 Attach the pillow extension to the towel by placing the raw edge even with the upper towel edge (Fig. 5–14). Sew the pillow side in place leaving the grommet side free.

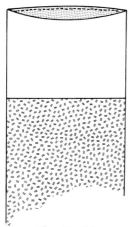

Fig. 5–14

8 Flip up the extension and stitch the grommet side to the towel only in places where there are no pillow openings (Fig. 5–15).

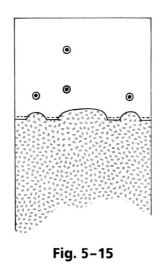

Fig. 5–15

SIDE EXTENSIONS

Directions

1 Now that you have your upper and lower extensions sewn to the towel, you can determine the new length of your towel for the side extensions. Using the long yardage of the leftover fabric, measure the new length of your towel and add ½ inch (12mm) for the seam allowance. Cut off a piece this length and the width of your leftovers. Cut the piece in half to make the two side extensions (Fig. 5–16).

Fig. 5–16

2 With right sides together, fold each strip in half lengthwise and seam the short ends (Fig. 5–17). Turn right side out and press. Press under one long raw edge ¼ inch (6mm) to the wrong side.

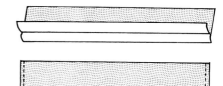

Fig. 5–17

3 Pin the unpressed raw edge of the extension to the right side of the towel and sew in place. The valves are on the wrong side (Fig. 5–18).

Fig. 5–18

4 From the back side, pin the extension to the towel and stitch in the ditch or sew in place by hand (Fig. 5–19). Repeat for other side.

Optional: If you would like a secret pocket compartment, slip a 7-inch (17.5cm) zipper in somewhere along the back side of a side extension before you stitch in the ditch. Sew across the top and bottom to prevent your items from sliding to the bottom of the towel.

To convert the towel back to a bag, fold the towel up and push it through the bottom, forcing the bag to turn right side out.

BEACH TOWEL COVER-UP

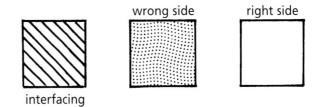

interfacing   wrong side   right side

Sew a Cover-Up from a towel with your favorite movie character on it or just mix and match solids with stripes. By strategically placing the pattern pieces, you can create some interesting effects. Nice features to have are snaps, a hood, and drawstring cords. With any luck there will be enough towel left over to make a matching tote bag. You can use your favorite jacket pattern, or follow the negative templates and hood pattern at the back of the book.

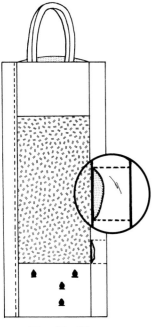

Fig. 5–19

These beach cover-ups can be made from your favorite towel. The matching tote has a zip open compartment in the bottom which is perfect for keeping wet things separate.

Please note that *all seams* are ½ inch (12mm). If you are using a serger, finish all raw edges first, then sew the seams using a ball point needle; otherwise, use the felled-seam technique. Before purchasing your towels, read these directions so that you will know how the towels will be cut up.

✓Materials

- ❍ Two beach towels approximately 30 × 60 inches (75 × 150cm)
- ❍ Six to eight snaps
- ❍ Four grommets
- ❍ 3½ yards (3.15m) of drawstring cord cut in two
- ❍ Interfacing for snap front and grommet areas

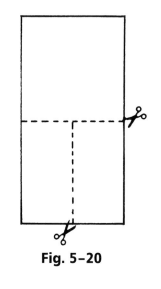

Fig. 5–20

Directions

These are approximate dimensions for a one-size-fits-all Cover-Up. Beach towels vary in size. If you are an extra-small person, you may want to trim some of the width. If you are an extra-large person, you may want to add to the width. One way of doing this is by facing the front snap area and hood separately. Our model includes a built-in facing, so you can use this to gain width. The front neck template is where you will find the facing. If you are adding a separate facing to your jacket, fold on the dotted lines to omit it; otherwise, just cut as is.

❶ Cut one towel in half the short way. Decide on a front and back. If necessary, use half from the second towel. Quite often existing borders can be used to create facings. Cut the front half up the middle to create a left and right half (Fig. 5–20). On our model, the two front halves are 15 × 30 inches (37.5 × 75cm) each. The back is 30 × 30 inches (75 × 75cm).

❷ On the front right half, place the front neck negative template in the upper right corner and cut the neck away. Repeat this for the front left half by putting the template on the upper left side and cutting the neck out (Fig. 5–21).

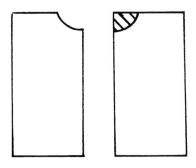

Fig. 5–21

❸ Fold the back piece in half, place the back neck negative template on the fold, and cut away the back neck (Figs. 5–22 and 5–23).

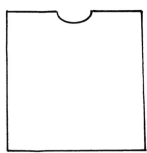

Fig. 5–22

Fig. 5–23

❹ For front and back shoulders, measure down 1 inch (2.5cm) on all pieces. Angle off the shoulder by drawing a line from the top of the neck to this mark. Cut it away (Figs. 5–24 and 5–25).

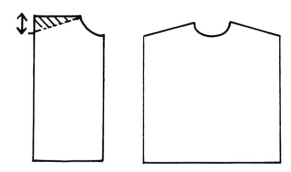

Fig. 5–24   **Fig. 5–25**

5 From the remaining towel, make sleeves and a hood. (Try to have a rectangle left over so that you can make a matching tote bag.) Cut four rectangles to form the sleeves (Fig. 5–26). For the sleeve hem, finished edges or borders are nice. You will need to estimate the length of your sleeve because this is a drop shoulder design. Simply hold one of the front sections to your body and see where the shoulder hits to decide on the length. Our sleeves worked out to be 15 inches (37.5cm) long and 11½ inches (28.75cm) wide.

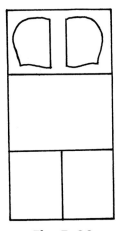

Fig. 5–26

6 With right sides together, sew the sleeves to the fronts and both sides of the back (Figs. 5–27 and 5–28).

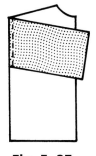

Fig. 5–27

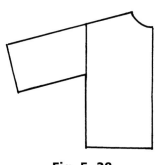

Fig. 5–28

7 With right sides together, sew the fronts to the back at shoulder/sleeve seams and underarm seams (Fig. 5–29).

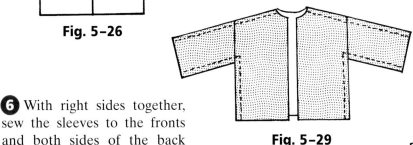

Fig. 5–29

8 Piece together the hood patterns from the back of the book, matching notches, and add 3¼ inches (8.2cm) to the front edge. Cut two hood sections from the leftover towel

fabric. Sew center-back seam of hood (Fig. 5–30).

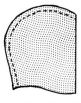

Fig. 5–30

9 Sew hood to jacket, matching center back with center-back seam of hood. Interface with a square of interfacing in the grommet areas and place grommets in hood and jacket bottom for drawstring. Fold the front edge of hood under ¼ inch (6mm) and then 1 inch (2.5cm) to form a drawstring casing. Hem the lower edge of Cover-Up to create a drawstring casing as well. Interface snap area and fold placket to wrong side. Topstitch in place. Evenly space five to six snaps. Set snaps. Insert drawstrings. With bias tape or leftover towel fabric, face the snap placket and hood. Place snaps and insert drawstring (Fig. 5–31).

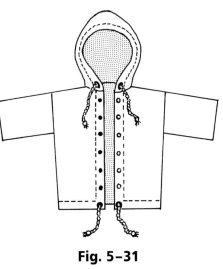

Fig. 5–31

Beach Towel Tote

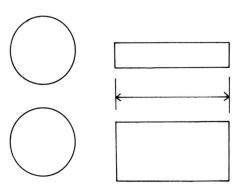

Fig. 5–32

The lower compartment of the Beach Towel Tote can be made out of laminated fabric for wet items. You can even insulate it if you like.

✓Materials

- ❍ Leftovers from Beach Towel Cover-Up or one towel approximately 30 × 15 inches (75 × 37.5cm)
- ❍ ½ yard (45cm) of laminated fabric, or laminate your own
- ❍ Eight extra-large grommets
- ❍ Zipper interfacing
- ❍ Thick cord (See instructions on how to make your own on pages 61–62.)

Preparation

If you are working with a leftover piece of toweling, you must determine the diameter of the bag bottom circles first. To calculate this, take the length of the towel section (which later becomes the circumference of the bag) × 3.14 and add ½ inch (12mm) for the seam allowance. Look around your house for circles with this diameter (Fig. 5–32). Garbage cans, buckets, pots, and plates work well. From the laminated fabric, cut two this size. If you wish to line the inside and conceal the seams, cut a total of four circles. (See Step 9.)

Directions

1 From laminated fabric, cut a gusset 5 inches (12.5cm) high and the same length as the leftover towel (12cm × bag length).

2 On the gusset determine the middle and draw a line down the center the same length as your zipper (Fig. 5–33). Cut a frame ¼ inch (6mm) to each side of this line. Pin zipper in this opening and sew in place (Fig. 5–34).

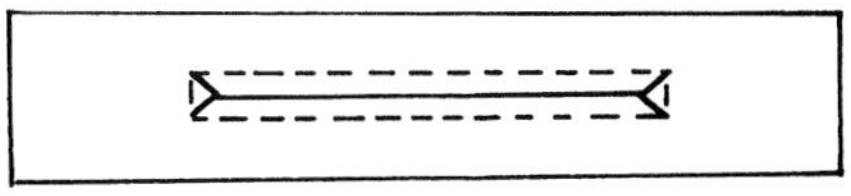

Fig. 5–33

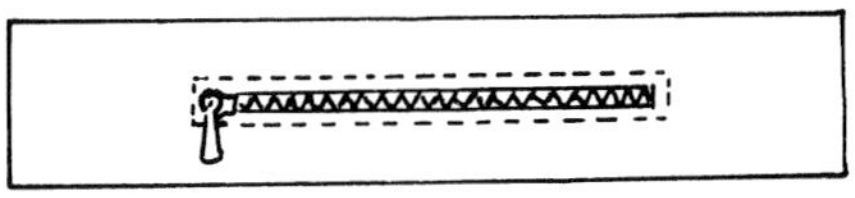

Fig. 5–34

❸ Close the center-back seam of the gusset. Pin gusset to the first circle, right sides together, and sew in place. This is the lower bag (Fig. 5–35).

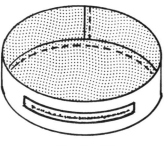

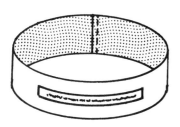

Fig. 5–35

❹ Interface the inside of the upper bag edge with a 1¾-inch-(4.38cm) wide strip of interfacing. Close upper bag to form a circle. Fold the upper edge toward the inside 2 inches (5cm) and topstitch in place. Evenly space and install eight extra-large grommets for the cord (Fig. 5–36).

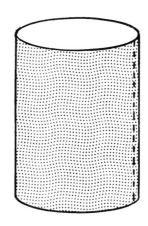

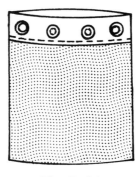

Fig. 5–36

❺ Baste a second circle to the bottom of upper bag. Bag should be right side out and wrong side of circle should be showing (Fig. 5–37). Do not sew yet.

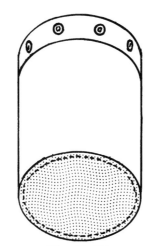

Fig. 5–37

❻ Purchase or make a thick cotton cord according to the instructions on pages 61–62. Weave it in and out through the grommets, starting and ending at center-back seam (Fig. 5–38). Pull cord even.

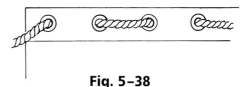

Fig. 5–38

❼ From a scrap piece, make a handle 5 × 8 inches (12.5 × 20cm). Hem upper and lower edge. With right sides together, fold in half and close the short side. Turn right side out and fold so that seam is in center back. Sew down the center (Fig. 5–39).

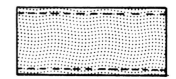

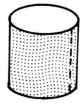

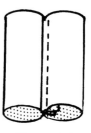

Fig. 5–39

8 Attach gusset portion to bag portion matching center back seam of bag with gusset seam. Slip each end of the cord through each handle opening. When pinning the gusset portion to the upper bag, be sure to insert the cord ends. Tuck the cord ends in between the upper bag and the gusset at center-back seam approximately 1 inch (2.5cm) to either side of the seam (Fig. 5–40).

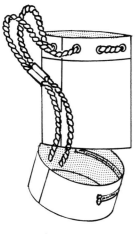

Fig. 5–40

9 Now, with right sides together, sew upper bag to gusset portion, matching center back seams (Fig. 5–41).

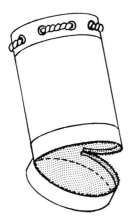

Fig. 5–41

10 If you wish to conceal the seams in the lower bag, place the two remaining circles right sides out in the bag bottoms, turning seam allowance of circles under. Sew in place by hand.

CORDING

It's easy to make your own beautiful cording using your favorite colors and yarns. This cord not only is suitable for drawstrings and purse handles but can also be used as decorative borders and couching. You will require a space three times the length of the cord you plan on making. A hallway, living room, or garage works well. A doorknob will be required if you are doing this by yourself; otherwise, a helper will be nec-

essary. Also, you will need a chair, two pairs of scissors, and a pencil.

Directions

1 In a space three times the length of the finished cord, tie one end of the yarn to a doorknob. Position a chair at the other end of the space. Wrap the yarn back and forth from the doorknob to around the chair leg until the yarn held together is half the desired thickness of the finished cord (Fig. 5–42).

2 Remove the yarn from the chair leg, and slip the yarn through one of the finger holes on a pair of scissors (Fig. 5–43).

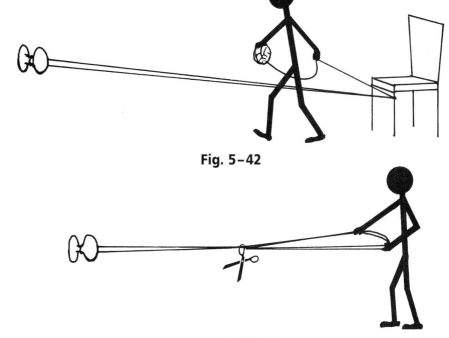

Fig. 5–42

Fig. 5–43

3 On the chair end stick a pencil in the middle of the yarn (Fig. 5–44).

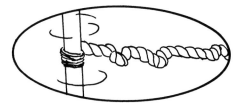

Fig. 5–46

Fig. 5–44

4 Turn the pencil in a circular fashion (like a propeller), twisting the yarn (Fig. 5–45). Twist for a long time until the yarn starts to knot up (Fig. 5–46). Remove the pencil.

5 Keeping everything taut, reach to grab the scissors and get the chair end over to the doorknob end. Do not let go of the scissors! The scissors will now be at one end (Fig. 5–47). With the other pair of scissors, cut the yarn from the doorknob end, still keeping everything taut.

Fig. 5–48

7 Cut scissors off of cording (Fig. 5–49). Put tape on the ends to prevent raveling until ready to use.

Fig. 5–47   **Fig. 5–49**

Fig. 5–45

6 Stand up on the chair with the scissors at the bottom acting as a weight. Let the scissors turn twisting the cord until it stops (Fig. 5–48). *Caution!* The scissors will fall open and twist rapidly. Make sure that no children or pets are close by.

CHAPTER 6

A QUICK FIX

Sometimes vacations, trips, or invitations come unexpectedly and you find yourself standing in front of your closet wondering what you're going to take or wear. There really isn't enough time to sew a new outfit—or is there?

LACE SKIRT

Grandma's beautiful crocheted tablecloth with that awful moth-eaten hole will finally come in handy. You never had the heart to throw it away because you just knew that some day you would be able to make something out of it. Well, in minutes you can transform it into a masterpiece. Or you can buy a tablecloth at an import store or a thrift shop. Such a tablecloth is usually available only in white and it may even have a few stains, so give it a face-lift with fabric dye. If you choose to line it, be sure and dye your lining at the same time. In place of lining it, you can wear leggings underneath.

✓Materials

- ○ One circular tablecloth approximately 60 to 80 inches (150 to 200cm) in diameter
- ○ Pencil and string for making radius
- ○ 2- to 3-inch- (5 to 7.5cm) wide decorative elastic for waistband
- ○ Lining twice the skirt length (optional)

Directions

❶ Measure your waist and divide this by 3. Add 1 inch (2.5cm). This is the diameter of the circle you are going to cut out. Divide by 2 for the radius (Fig. 6–1).

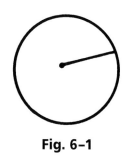

Fig. 6–1

❷ Find the center of the tablecloth, and transfer the radius by using a pencil and a string. The distance from the center of the tablecloth to the pencil should equal the radius. Draw a circle (Fig. 6–2).

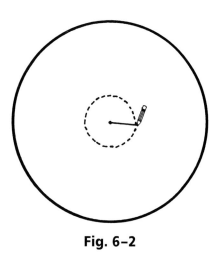

Fig. 6–2

❸ Before cutting out the circle, sew using a zigzag stitch all around the outside of the circle, taking care not to stretch anything out. Carefully cut away the center circle on the inside of the zigzag stitching (Fig. 6–3). If you own a serger, you should finish the raw edge one more time. Otherwise, zigzag again, taking care not to stretch the opening.

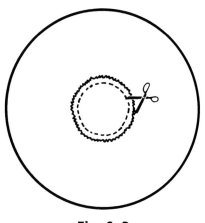

Fig. 6–3

4 Seam the decorative elastic together so that it comfortably fits your waist. Make quarter markers with pins on both the elastic and the skirt. Pin the elastic to the outside of the skirt, stretching it to match the markers. Topstitch the elastic in place (Fig. 6–4).

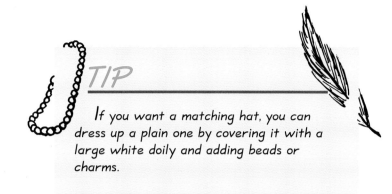

TIP

If you want a matching hat, you can dress up a plain one by covering it with a large white doily and adding beads or charms.

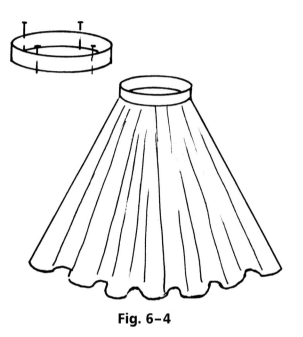

Fig. 6–4

CHARMING DOILY T-SHIRT

Adding doilies to a plain T-shirt is a quick way
to sew and go.

An inexpensive plain T-shirt can be embellished easily and quickly with four to five small doilies. Arrange them around the front neckline overlapping each other. This will create a new, lower neckline.

Directions

1 Position the doilies along the front of the shirt, keeping in mind that you are creating a new neckline. Decide how high or low you wish to go with your neckline. Pin and then zigzag in a spiral fashion around each doily, securing it in place (Fig. 6–5).

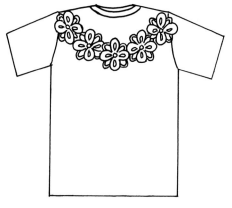

Fig. 6–5

2 Cut out the new neckline along the doily edges (Fig. 6–6). Trim away the ribbing, and the neck in the back will just roll under. T-shirts are usually made of interlock, so fraying should not be a problem. (There are solutions available on the market that can be applied to the raw edges to prevent fraying if it occurs.)

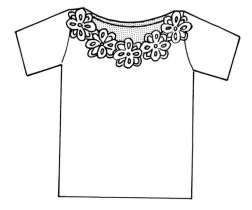

Fig. 6–6

If you wish to state your love for sewing, attach a few sewing-related charms to the doilies.

BEADED FRINGE

Embellish garments and create attractive accessories from fringe beaded with wooden animals, shells, bells, and glass and silver beads.

the twill tape to the underside of the garment, for example, under the front opening of a vest (Fig. 6–8).

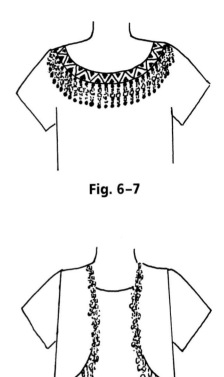

Fig. 6–7

Fig. 6–8

You have seen it on all the designer-wear clothing in the stores. It's exciting, new, and fun to wear. Beaded fringe is now available to the home sewer by the yard, and the choices include glass beads, wooden animals, shells, seed beads, silver beads, and bells. There's no better way to create a quick fix than with beaded fringe. If you look far back enough into your closet, you will probably find a few classic stand-bys, such as blazers, skirts, and tops, that aren't really out of style but just don't excite you anymore. Well, it's beaded fringe to the rescue. Somebody has already spent time-consuming hours stringing beads and attaching them to twill tape or woven ribbon. All you have to do is buy some by the yard and go wild. It's the fastest way to give a garment a face-lift, and the results will be stunning! About 2 yards (1.8m) should do the trick. Buy extra fringe and make a pair of matching earrings and a hair barrette.

Beaded fringe can be attached in three ways:

1. Use the decorative ribbon and topstitch the beaded fringe directly to the outside of the garment (Fig. 6–7), or sew

2. Incorporate the tape between seams so that it is concealed. Only the beaded fringe is dangling down. This is probably the most attractive version. You can cut new seams to create a place to conceal the tape such as at the bottom of a shirt or blouse. It is most attractive when the beading ends just before it hits the hemline. Place the fringe facing upward on the right side of the garment. Place cutoff garment section on top, sandwiching the fringe in between.

Sew concealing the tape (Figs. 6–9, 6–10, and 6–11).

Fig. 6–9

Fig. 6–10

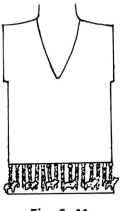

Fig. 6–11

3. If you are in a terrible hurry, pull out the glue gun and glue the fringe on where it won't be seen.

ACCESSORIES

Accessories are the *hinges* to our wardrobe. They make our outfits special and unique. Here are a few quick fixes to make with the leftover fringe.

HAIR BARRETTE

Directions

1 Measure the length of the hair barrette (Fig. 6–12).

Fig. 6–12

2 Take the beaded fringe and roll it up approximately five to six times, using the length of the barrette as your measurement (Fig. 6–13).

Fig. 6–13

3 Stitch through the layers of fringe to hold it in place and keep it from unrolling (Fig. 6–14).

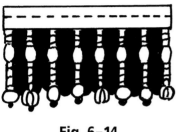

Fig. 6–14

4 Hot glue gun the beaded roll to the barrette, turning the twill tape so that it makes the beads face upward (Fig. 6–15).

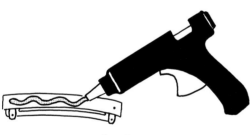

Fig. 6–15

EARRINGS

Directions

1 Roll the twill tape in a tight roll with the beads hanging down until it forms a full cluster (Fig. 6–16).

Fig. 6–16

2 Hot glue gun the cluster to some earring clips, turning the twill tape so that the beads hide the clip and tape (Fig. 6–17). If you wish to make wire earrings, you can restring the beads onto some jewelry wire and then attach them to a pair of wire earrings.

Fig. 6–17

TIP

Look for other items to embellish with, such as silk ribbon roses and fringe with wooden animals. There are no limitations.

CHAPTER 7

Memories

TRAVEL JOURNALS, DIARIES, AND SCRAPBOOKS

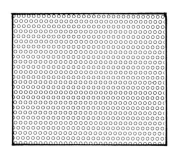

Keeping a travel journal is a wonderful way to keep memories fresh. Scrapbooks are the perfect way to reminisce. Whether they're brochures, photos, or any other traveling treasures you wish to keep, you'll enjoy looking through them over and over again. Hand-made fabric-covered journals, diaries, and scrapbooks become even more special. Give them as bon voyage gifts. Let your children participate in the making of the books, and talk about what they can collect and what they might see.

Fig. 7–1

Keep the kids from getting bored on vacation with a variety of take-along projects including travel journals, diaries, and scrapbooks. (See Chapter 5 for other entertainment ideas.)

2 Iron HeatnBond to wrong side of the larger fabric. Trim fabric back to HeatnBond edges. Peel away paper protector sheet. Center notebook on fabric, and from fabric side iron the front cover first, then spine, and then back cover (Figs. 7–2 and 7–3)

DIARY OR TRAVEL JOURNAL

✓ Materials

○ Notebook

○ Fabric slightly larger than opened book

○ Two pieces of fabric slightly smaller than cover

○ Double-sided fusible iron-on HeatnBond

○ Colored paper for inside lining (optional)

Directions

1 Measure length and width of cover and spine. Add 1½ inches (3.75cm) all around. Cut a piece of HeatnBond this size (Fig. 7–1).

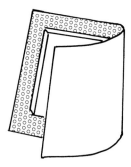

Fig. 7–2

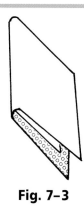

Fig. 7–3

3 Cut in at an angle at top and bottom of spine. Cut away squares at each corner (Fig. 7–4). Fold in each side flap and iron it in place. Trim off excess at spine.

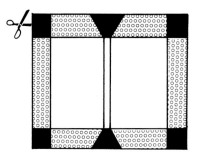

Fig. 7–4

4 With another piece of fabric slightly smaller than the cover itself, line the inside front cover to conceal the raw edges of the turned-over fabric. Cut and fuse HeatnBond as you did in Steps 1 and 2. Do the same to the inside back cover. You can also line the inside with good-quality colored paper (Fig. 7–5).

Fig. 7–5

SCRAPBOOK

✓ Materials

- ❍ Two pieces of sturdy cardboard cut to the size of the paper you will be filling the scrapbook with
- ❍ Fabric large enough to cover two pieces of cardboard and line the inside
- ❍ Six extra-large grommets
- ❍ HeatnBond to cover both covers
- ❍ One package of colored construction paper

Directions

1 Score cardboard for front cover 1½ inches (3.75cm) in from one edge and fold it back. Do the same for the back cover.

2 Cut two pieces of HeatnBond 1½ inches (3.75cm) all around larger than the cardboard covers. Iron HeatnBond to fabric. Trim fabric back to size of HeatnBond (Fig. 7–6).

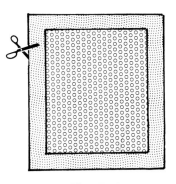

Fig. 7–6

3 Iron fabric to cardboard cover, taking care not to iron past the cardboard (Fig. 7-7).

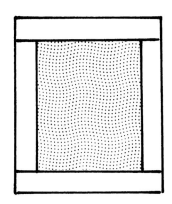

Fig. 7–7

4 Cut square away at each corner of fabric (Fig. 7–8). Iron loose flaps toward the wrong side.

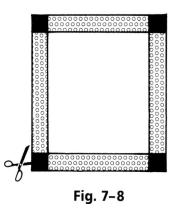

Fig. 7–8

5 Space and install three grommets on each cover (Fig. 7–9). If you are using paper with holes, space grommets to match holes.

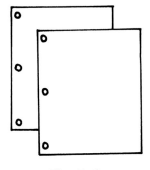

Fig. 7–9

6 Use a standard paper punch to punch holes in the colored construction paper (Fig. 7–10). Fill the book with the paper. Tie together with ribbon, shoelaces, leather, or matching fabric strips (Fig. 7–11).

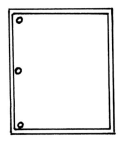

inside of cover

Fig. 7–10

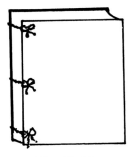

Fig. 7–11

COLLECT-A-STATE

Learn geography the fun way! Start by tracing a map of the United States onto a piece of muslin (see pattern at the back of the book). You can collect a new state every time you go somewhere, have a friend move, visit grandparents, etc. Trace the desired state onto a brightly colored piece of fabric and iron it to the muslin map. Later you can sew the map to a pillowcase, jacket, placemat, or wall quilt. You'll be impressed with how well your child will remember the shapes of the different states as well as their locations. Learn the fun way—one piece at a time!

Directions

1 Iron Wonder-Under to a piece of muslin large enough to accommodate the entire United States map.

2 Tape the paper pattern together at the center. Trace the map of the United States and outline all fifty states as shown on the master pattern.

3 Cut out the map. At this point you can pin your map to a bulletin board or iron it to a larger piece of fabric. Each time you collect a state, trace the state's shape onto a piece of fabric with Wonder-Under on the back and iron it in place on the map. If you plan to make a quilt, you can embroider dates and travel paths on the fabric states.

Patterns and Templates

front

cut 2 on fold

fold

open

Laundry Kit

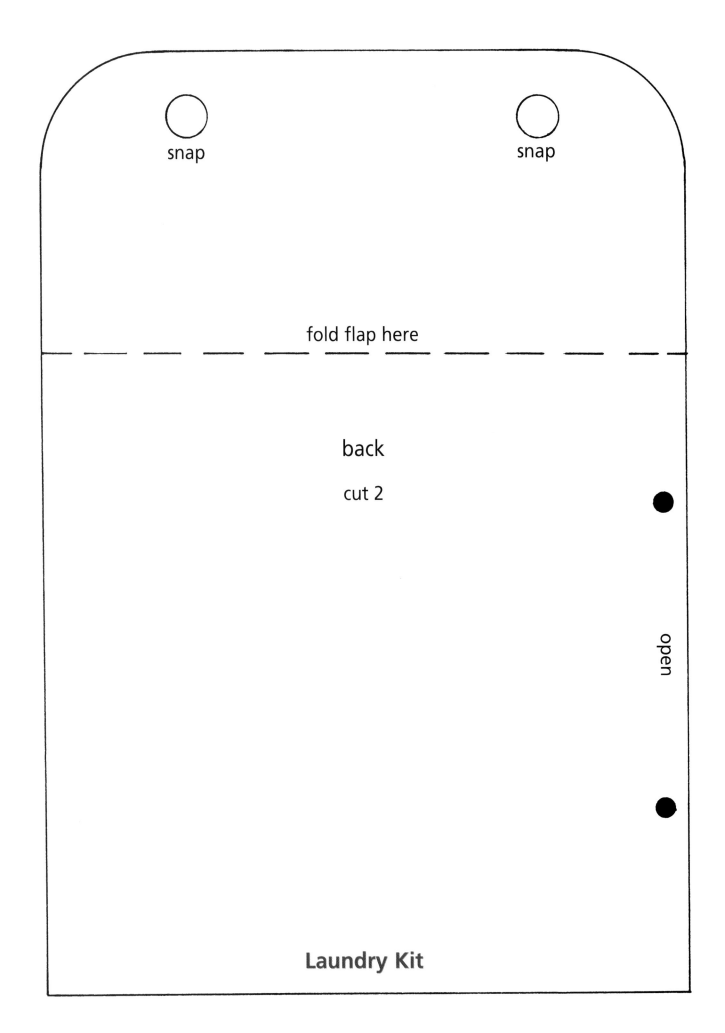

snap

snap

fold flap here

back

cut 2

open

Laundry Kit

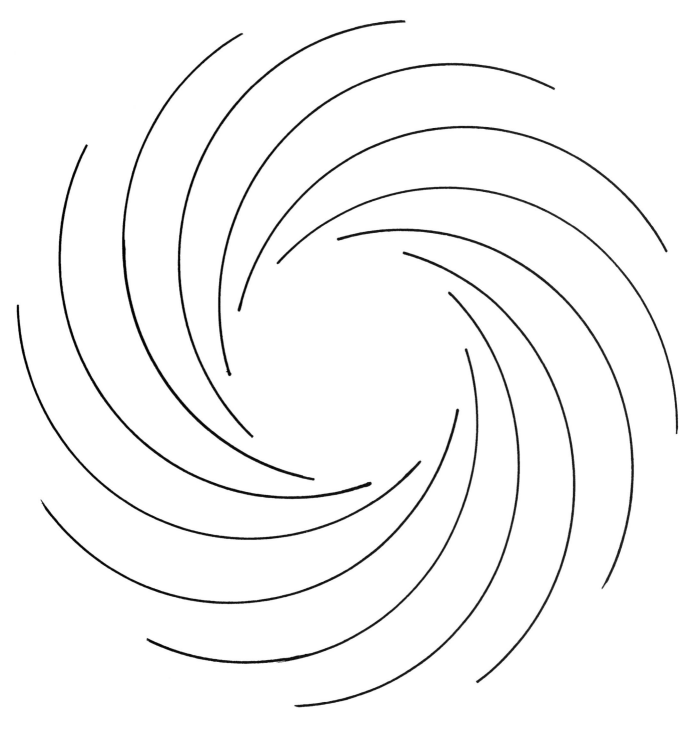

Flat Hat Template
transfer and cut

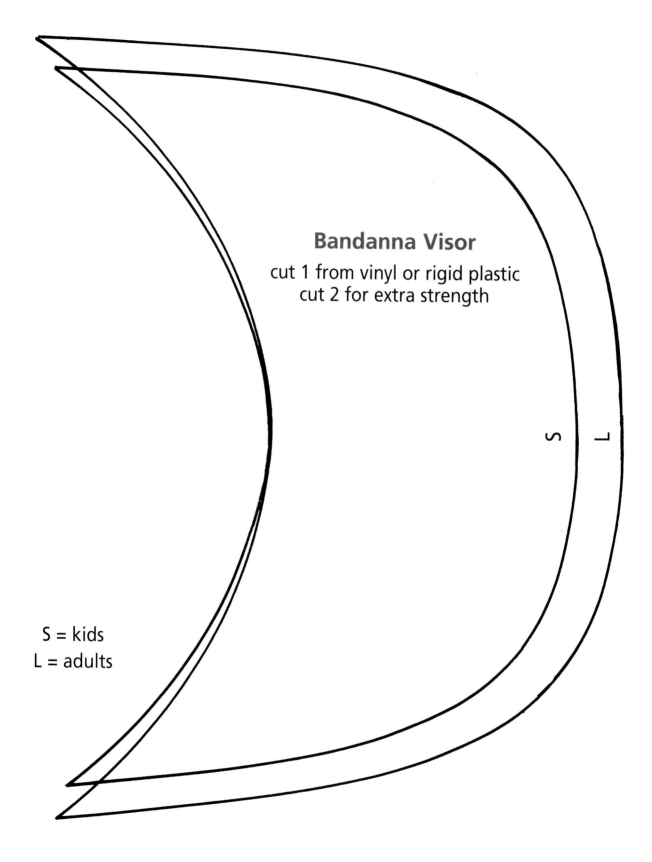

Bandanna Visor
cut 1 from vinyl or rigid plastic
cut 2 for extra strength

S

L

S = kids
L = adults

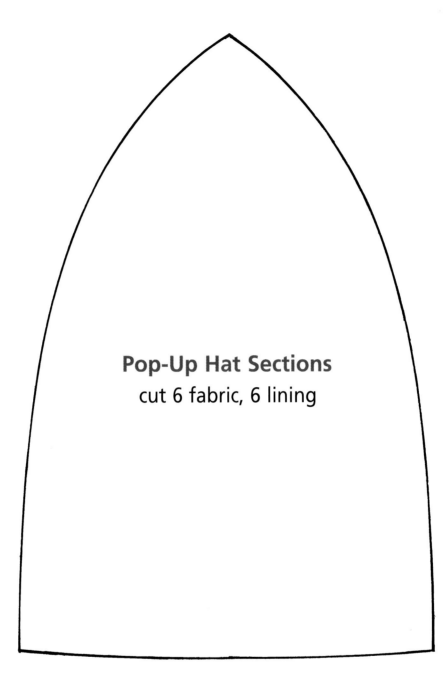

Pop-Up Hat Sections
cut 6 fabric, 6 lining

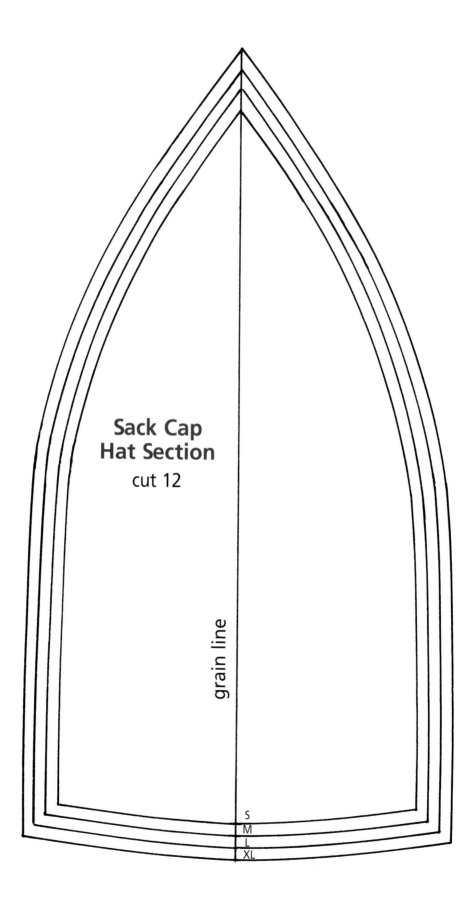

Sack Cap
Hat Section
cut 12

grain line

S
M
L
XL

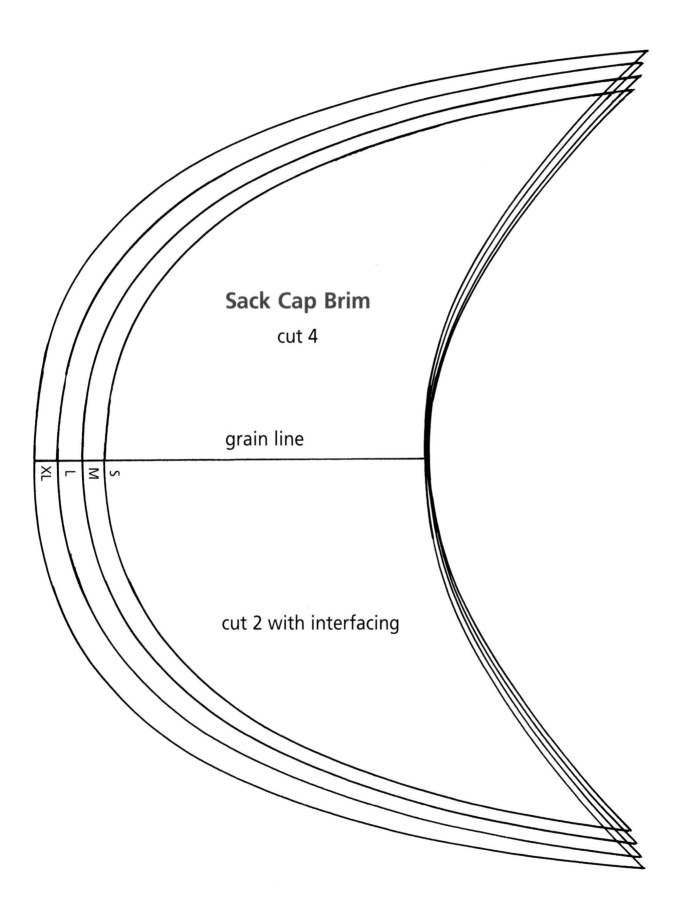

Sack Cap Brim

cut 4

grain line

XL L M S

cut 2 with interfacing

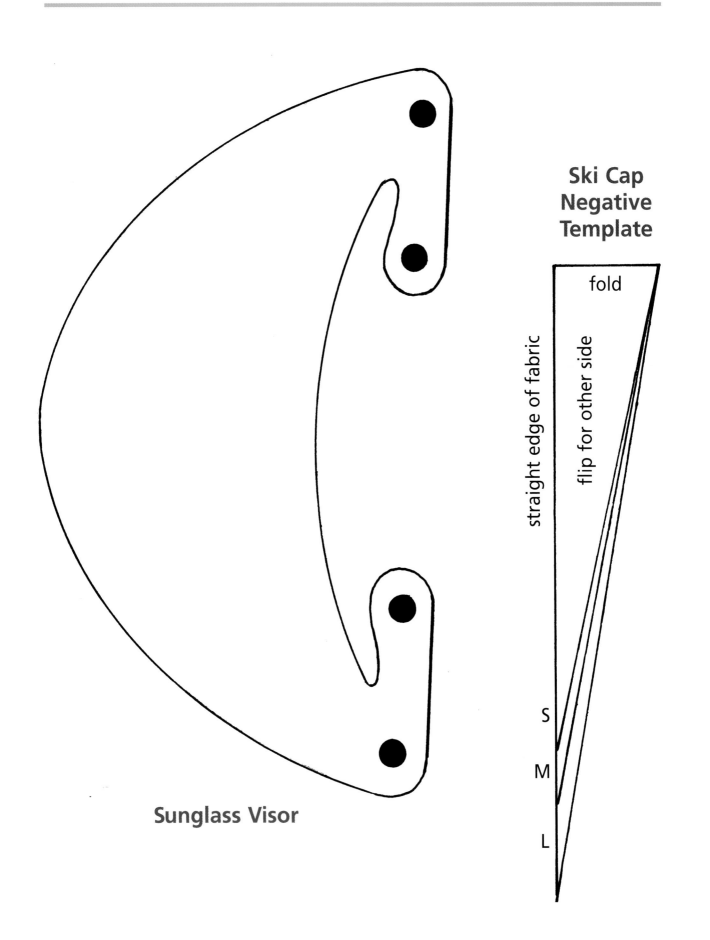

Ski Cap Negative Template

fold

straight edge of fabric

flip for other side

S

M

L

Sunglass Visor

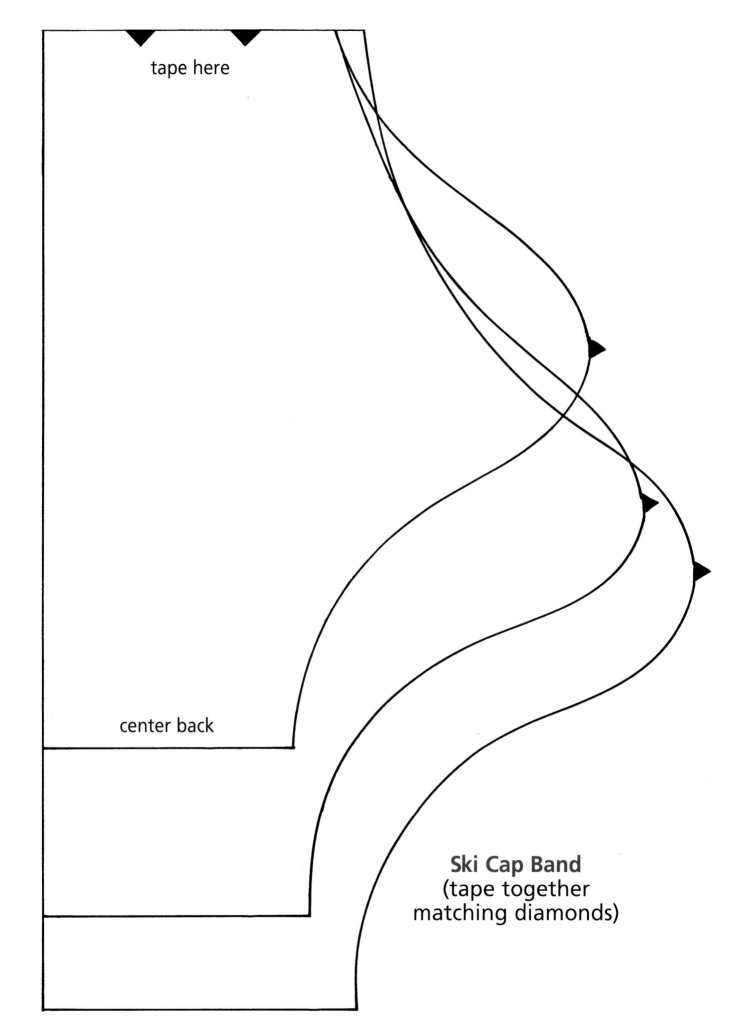

tape here

center back

Ski Cap Band
(tape together
matching diamonds)

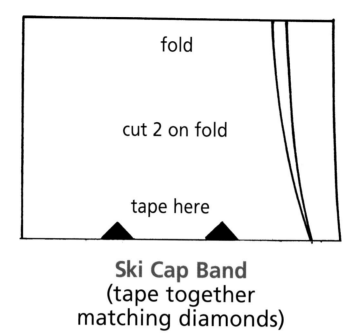

Ski Cap Band
(tape together
matching diamonds)

Standard Backpack Pocket Flap

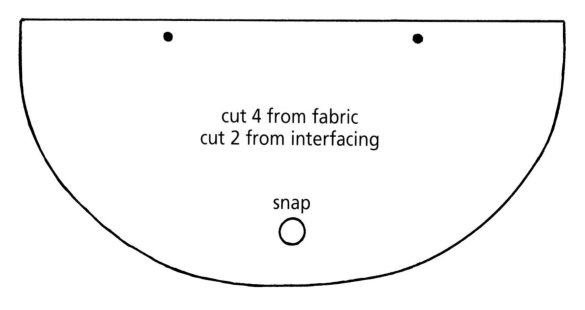

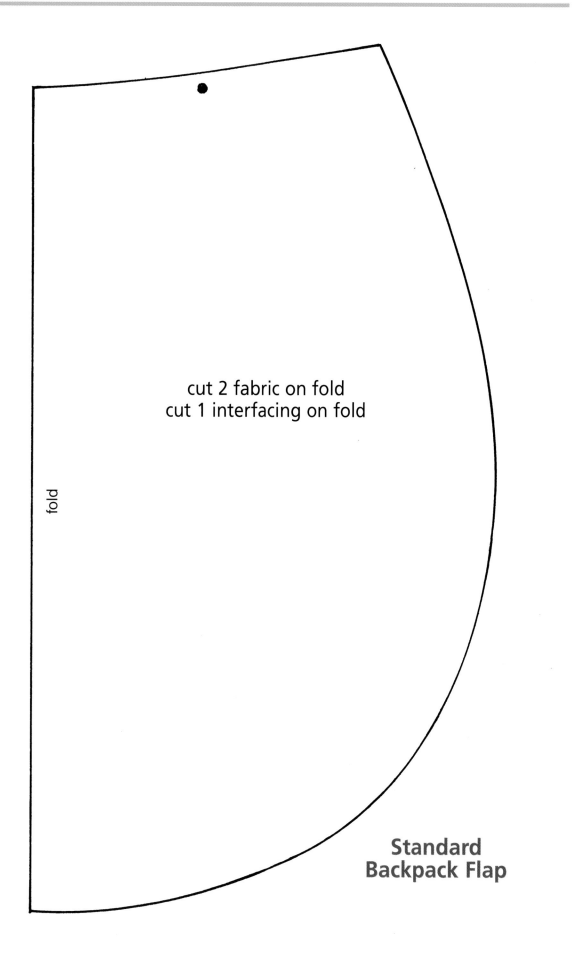

cut 2 fabric on fold
cut 1 interfacing on fold

fold

**Standard
Backpack Flap**

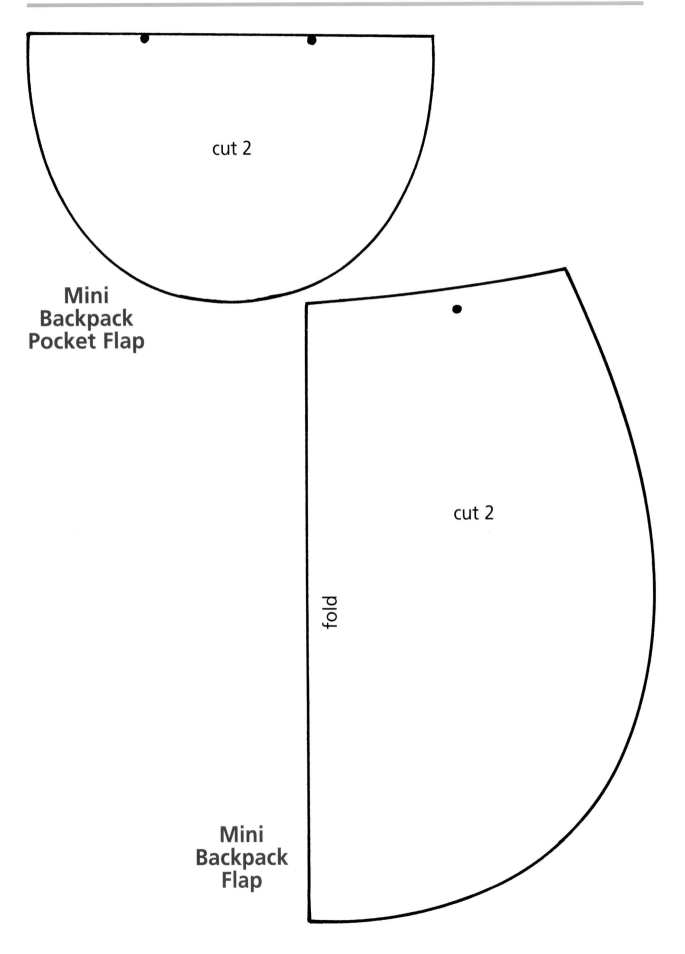

**Mini
Backpack
Pocket Flap**

cut 2

cut 2

fold

**Mini
Backpack
Flap**

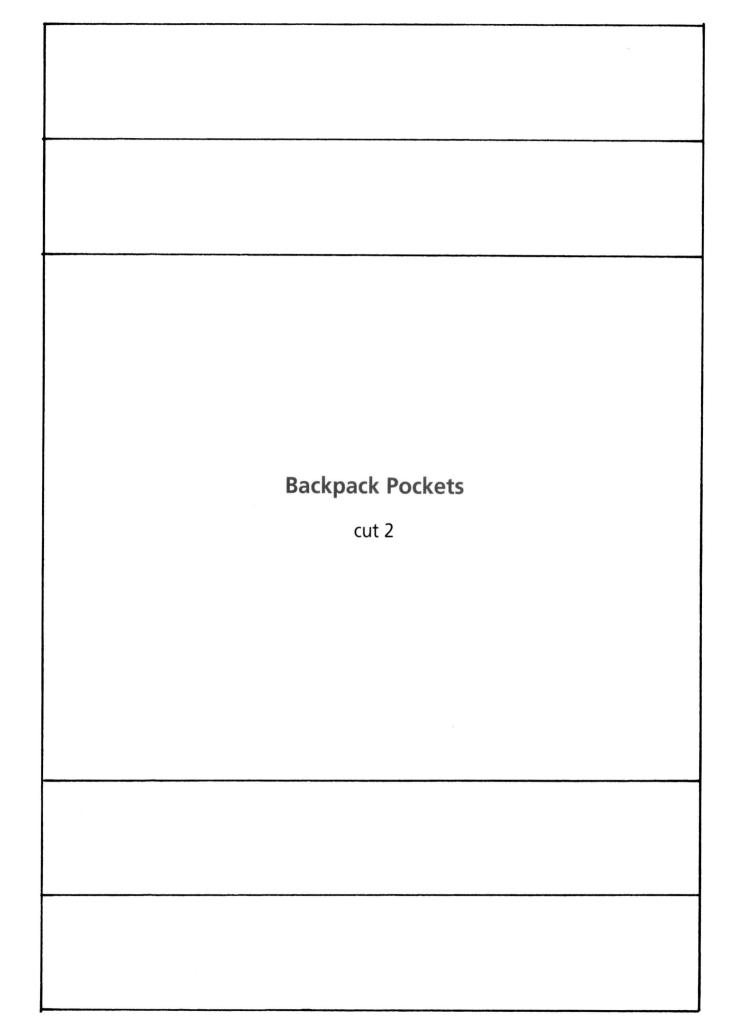

Backpack Pockets

cut 2

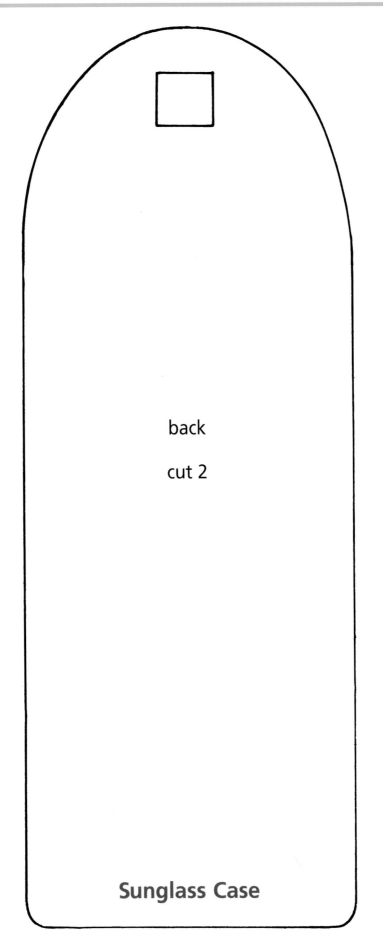

back

cut 2

Sunglass Case

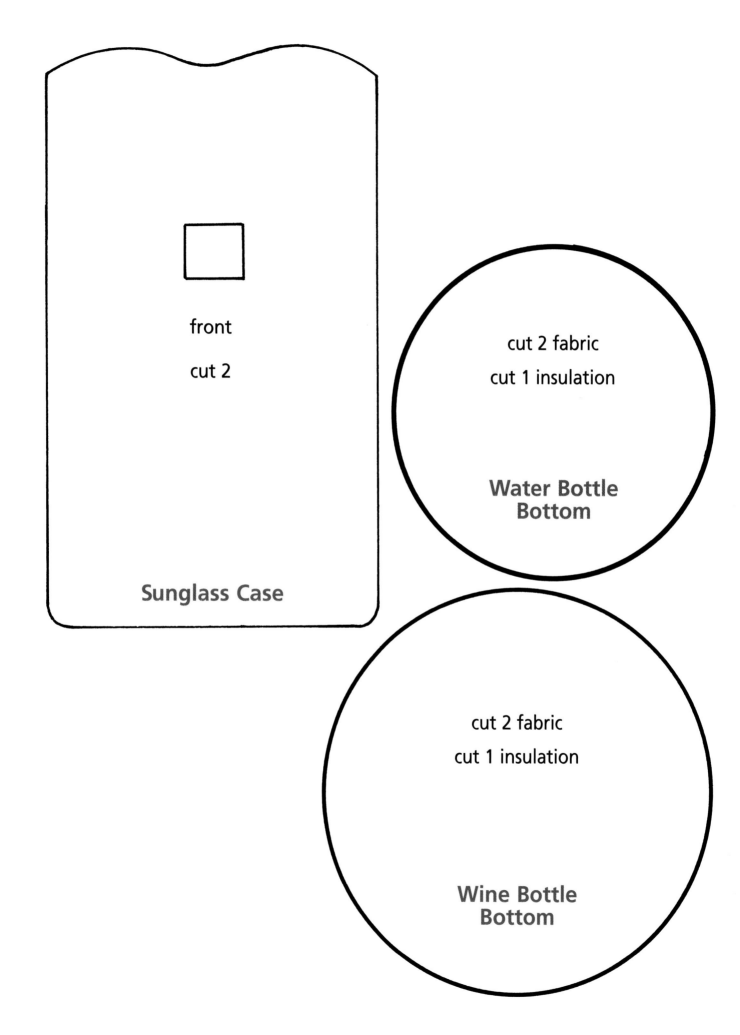

front

cut 2

Sunglass Case

cut 2 fabric

cut 1 insulation

Water Bottle Bottom

cut 2 fabric

cut 1 insulation

Wine Bottle Bottom

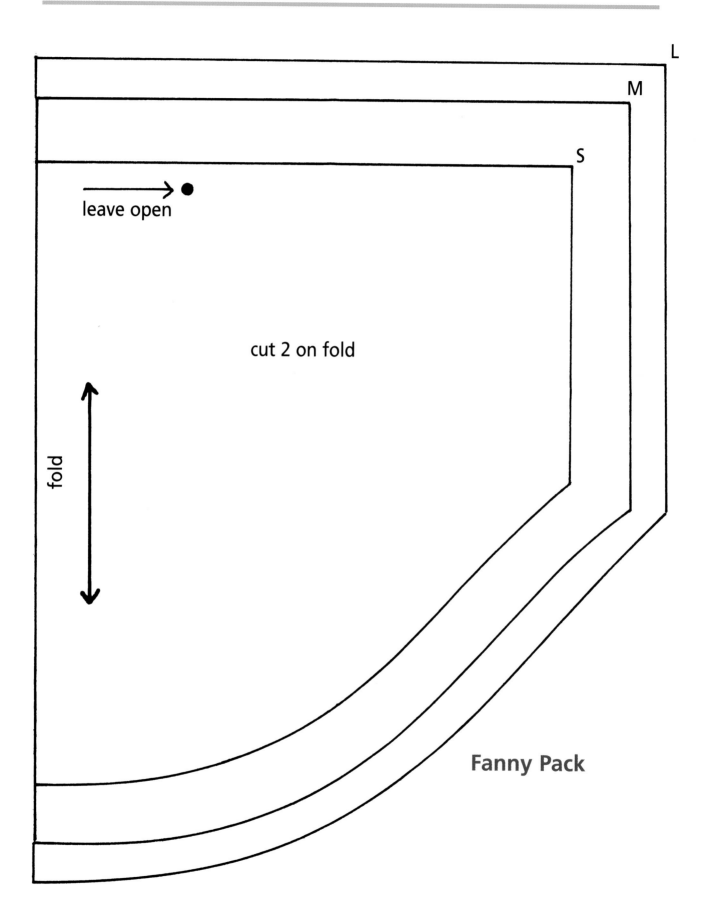

L

M

S

leave open

cut 2 on fold

fold

Fanny Pack

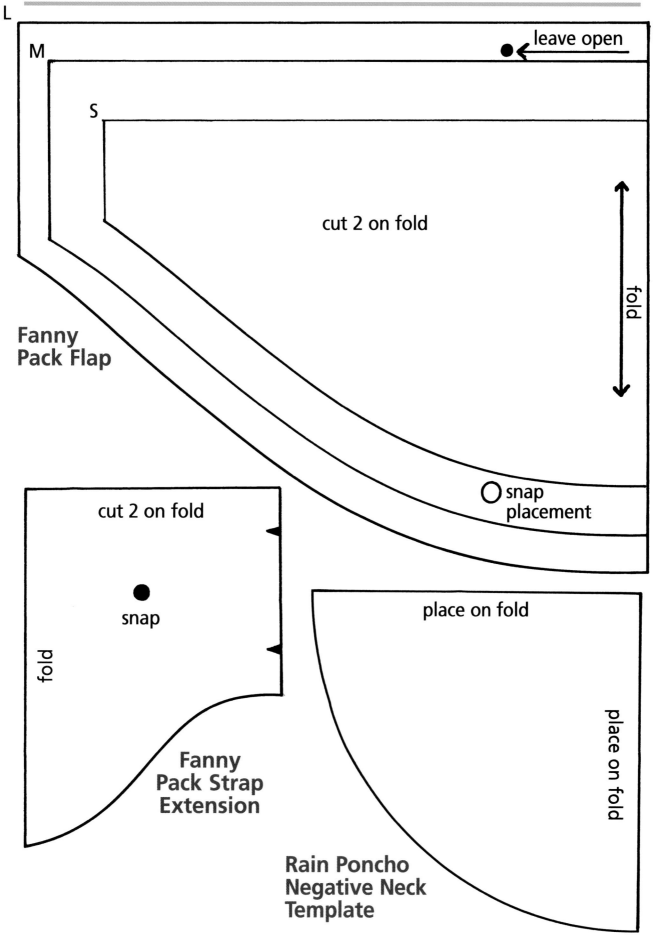

L

M

S

leave open

cut 2 on fold

fold

Fanny
Pack Flap

snap
placement

cut 2 on fold

snap

fold

Fanny
Pack Strap
Extension

place on fold

place on fold

Rain Poncho
Negative Neck
Template

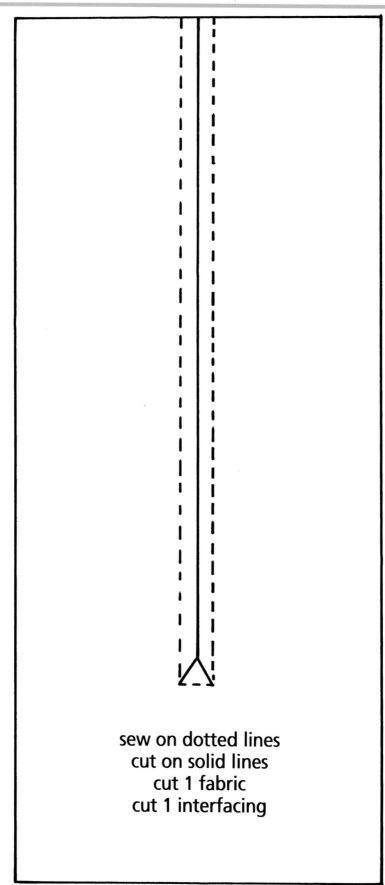

sew on dotted lines
cut on solid lines
cut 1 fabric
cut 1 interfacing

Rain Poncho Zipper Placket

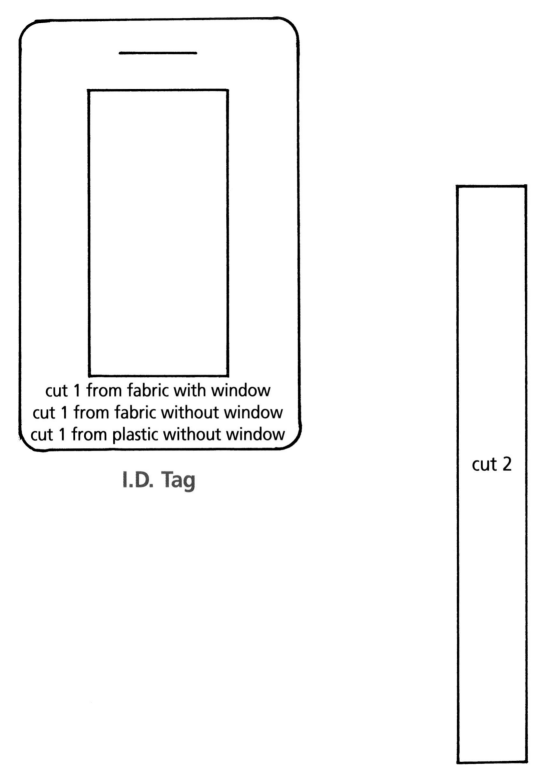

cut 1 from fabric with window
cut 1 from fabric without window
cut 1 from plastic without window

I.D. Tag

cut 2

I.D. Tag Strap

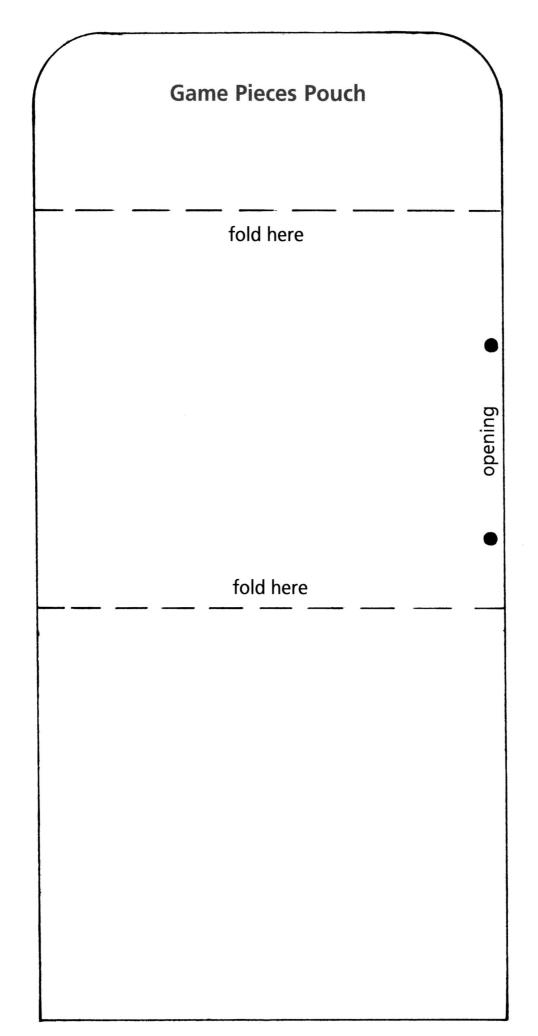

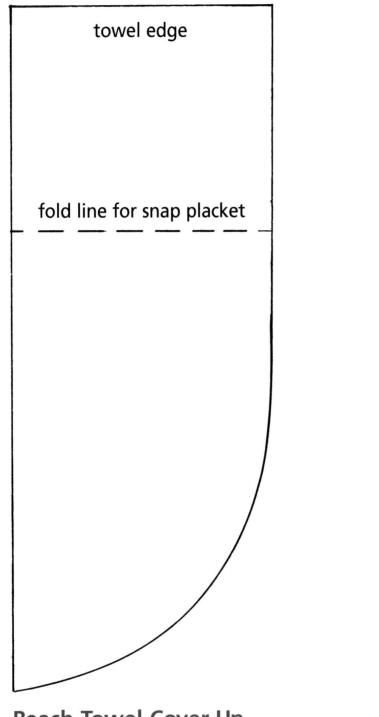

towel edge

fold line for snap placket

**Beach Towel Cover-Up
Negative Template
for Front Neck**

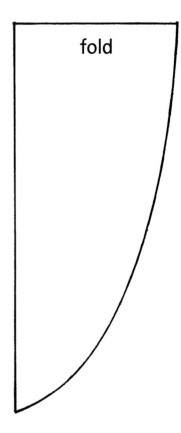

fold

**Beach Towel
Cover-Up Negative
Template
for Back Neck**

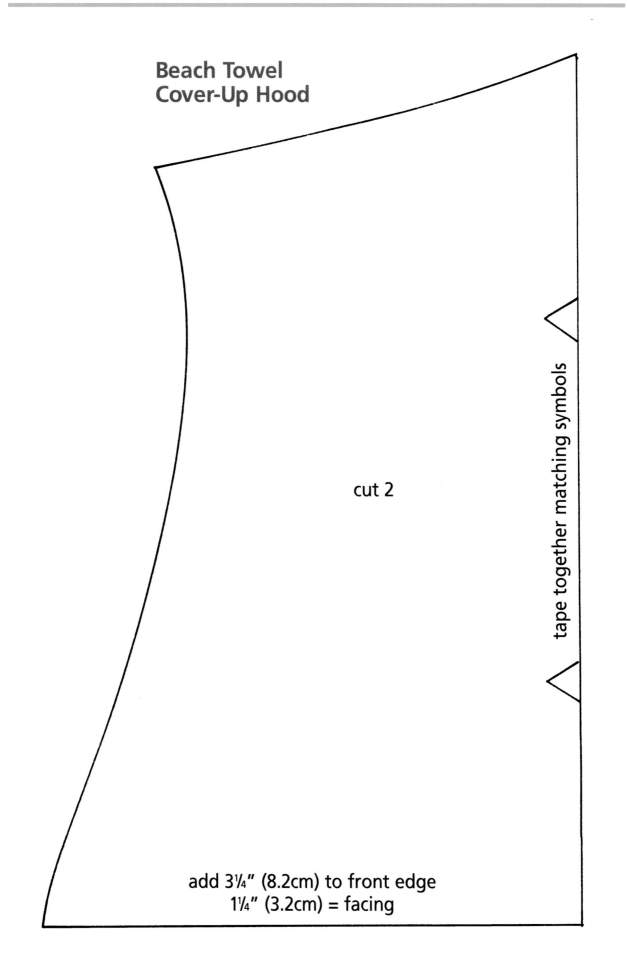

**Beach Towel
Cover-Up Hood**

cut 2

tape together matching symbols

add 3¼" (8.2cm) to front edge
1¼" (3.2cm) = facing

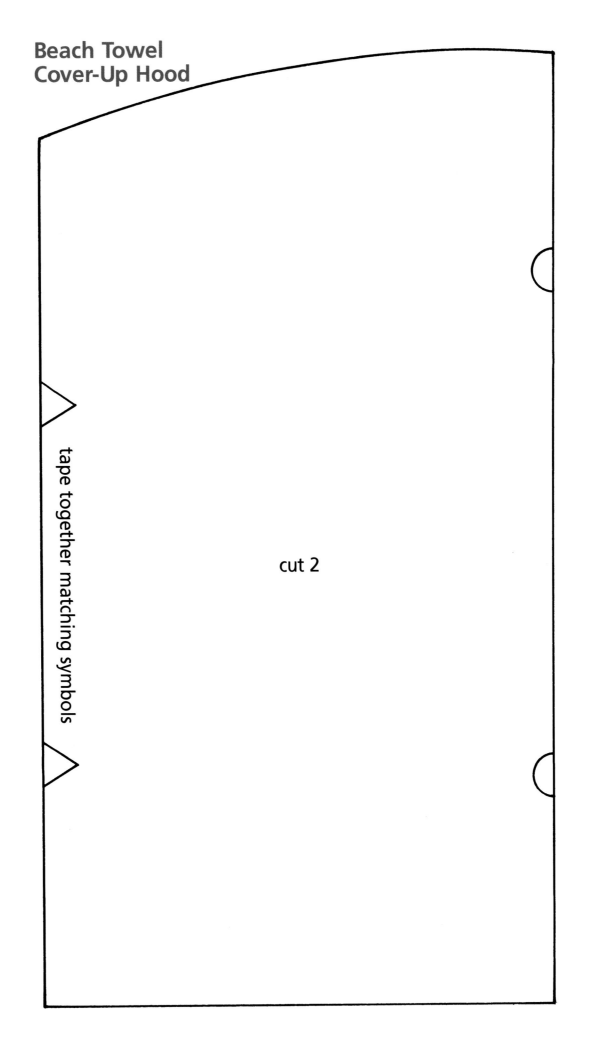

Beach Towel Cover-Up Hood

tape together matching symbols

cut 2

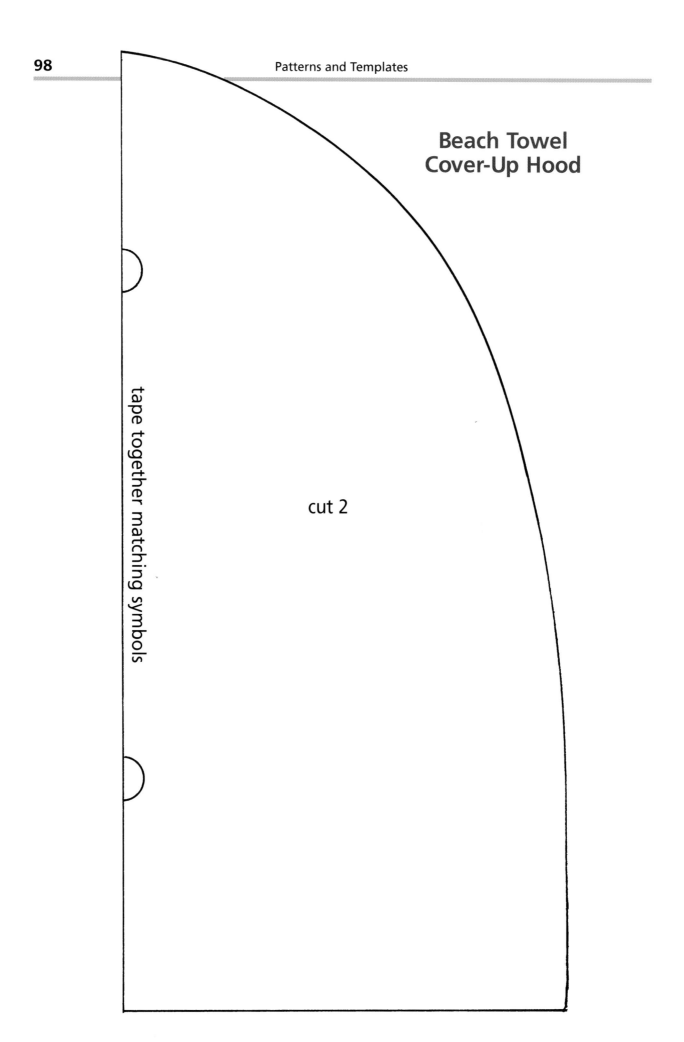

**Beach Towel
Cover-Up Hood**

tape together matching symbols

cut 2

Collect-a-State

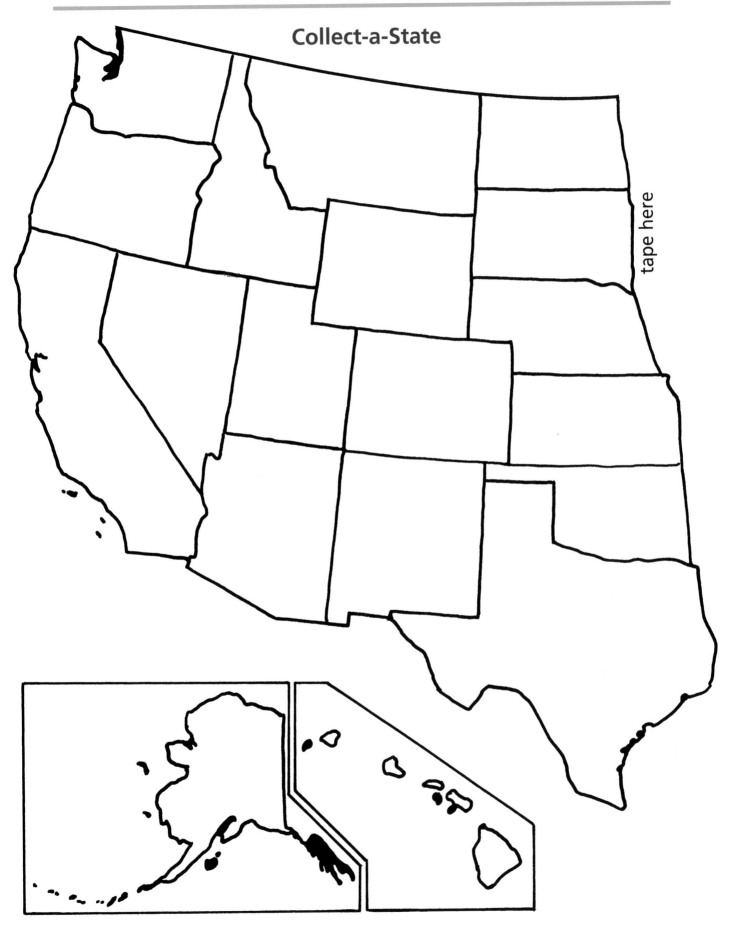

tape here

Collect-a-State

tape here

Resources

✓ **Beaded Fringe**

South Beach Trimmings

    P.O. Box 12009-652

    Scottsdale, AZ 85267

    Mail-order catalog,
    $2.00

✓ **Sewing Charms**

Deborah Gayle

    P.O. Box 402

    Rodeo, CA 94572

    1-800-484-9922

✓ **Snaps and Grommets**

The Snap Queen

    P.O. Box 6901

    San Mateo, CA 94403

    Catalog upon request
    1-800-736-0854

✓ **Patterns**

Birch Street Clothing

    P.O. Box 6901

    San Mateo, CA 94403

    Catalog upon request
    1-800-736-0854

✓ **HeatnBond Iron-on Flexible Vinyl**

Thermo Web Inc.

    Dept. VC

    770 Glenn Ave.

    Wheeling, IL 60090

    Available in most fabric
    stores

✓ **Laminated Fabrics**

Rain Shed

    707 N.W. 11th St.

    Corvallis, OR 97330

✓ **Fabulous Furs and Fabu-Leather**

Donna Salyers

    700 Madison Ave.

    Covington, KY 41011

✓ **Supplex and Ultrex and Other Outdoor Fabrics**

Seattle Fabrics

    3876 Bridge Way North

    Seattle, WA 98103

    206-632-6022

Index